LAW, CRIME AND LAW ENFORCEMENT

AF678857

JUVENILE DELINQUENCY

CAUSES, CONTROL AND CONSEQUENCES

LAW, CRIME AND LAW ENFORCEMENT

Additional books in this series can be found on Nova's website under the Series tab.

Additional e-books in this series can be found on Nova's website under the e-books tab.

LAW, CRIME AND LAW ENFORCEMENT

JUVENILE DELINQUENCY

CAUSES, CONTROL AND CONSEQUENCES

BONNIE A. NELSON
EDITOR

NOVINKA
New York

Copyright © 2016 by Nova Science Publishers, Inc.

All rights reserved. No part of this book may be reproduced, stored in a retrieval system or transmitted in any form or by any means: electronic, electrostatic, magnetic, tape, mechanical photocopying, recording or otherwise without the written permission of the Publisher.

We have partnered with Copyright Clearance Center to make it easy for you to obtain permissions to reuse content from this publication. Simply navigate to this publication's page on Nova's website and locate the "Get Permission" button below the title description. This button is linked directly to the title's permission page on copyright.com. Alternatively, you can visit copyright.com and search by title, ISBN, or ISSN.

For further questions about using the service on copyright.com, please contact:
Copyright Clearance Center
Phone: +1-(978) 750-8400 Fax: +1-(978) 750-4470 E-mail: info@copyright.com.

NOTICE TO THE READER

The Publisher has taken reasonable care in the preparation of this book, but makes no expressed or implied warranty of any kind and assumes no responsibility for any errors or omissions. No liability is assumed for incidental or consequential damages in connection with or arising out of information contained in this book. The Publisher shall not be liable for any special, consequential, or exemplary damages resulting, in whole or in part, from the readers' use of, or reliance upon, this material. Any parts of this book based on government reports are so indicated and copyright is claimed for those parts to the extent applicable to compilations of such works.

Independent verification should be sought for any data, advice or recommendations contained in this book. In addition, no responsibility is assumed by the publisher for any injury and/or damage to persons or property arising from any methods, products, instructions, ideas or otherwise contained in this publication.

This publication is designed to provide accurate and authoritative information with regard to the subject matter covered herein. It is sold with the clear understanding that the Publisher is not engaged in rendering legal or any other professional services. If legal or any other expert assistance is required, the services of a competent person should be sought. FROM A DECLARATION OF PARTICIPANTS JOINTLY ADOPTED BY A COMMITTEE OF THE AMERICAN BAR ASSOCIATION AND A COMMITTEE OF PUBLISHERS.

Additional color graphics may be available in the e-book version of this book.

Library of Congress Cataloging-in-Publication Data

ISBN: 978-1-63485-742-0

Published by Nova Science Publishers, Inc. † New York

CONTENTS

PREFACE

This book focuses on the causes, control and consequences of juvenile delinquency. Chapter One begins with an overview of the social, cultural and interpersonal issues with justice involved adolescents. Chapter Two's purpose is to help understand the major developmental theorist's view of critical developmental milestones, understand the social, biological and interpersonal effects on an adolescents' functioning; learn how rage, anger and delinquency are central components in the developing adolescents' skills to manage behavioral outbursts; identify aspects of depression and anxiety in adolescents and how these symptoms manifest into pathology; learn skills and tools to work with adolescents who struggle with these changes and adolescents who are defiant to the therapy process; identify markers related to low and inflated self-esteem and how it may disrupt adolescent development; improve awareness of friendship development and group identity contribute and its impact on decision making; and identify ethical and other best practice implications. Chapter Three studies the construction of juvenile restorative justice in Italy and Chile, how these policies are implemented in practice, and how families participate in these processes. Chapter Four discusses youth transitions and social exclusion through an empirical study of young ex-offenders' reintegration in China.

In: Juvenile Delinquency
Editor: Bonnie A. Nelson
ISBN: 978-1-63485-742-0
© 2016 Nova Science Publishers, Inc.

Chapter 1

SOCIAL, CULTURAL AND INTERPERSONAL ISSUES WITH JUSTICE INVOLVED ADOLESCENTS

Frances L. Dailey*, Lee A. Underwood†, Aryssa Washington‡ and Teri Hourihan§
Regent University, Virginia Beach, VA, US

Anthropologist Margaret Mead contributed to the field of adolescent development through her observations and interviews of Samoan adolescent girls. She wanted to discover whether puberty was as "stressful" for adolescents in Samoa, as it was for American adolescents (Zheng, 1999). After nine months, she concluded that the life of Samoan adolescents was less stressful because of their engagement in premarital sex (Feinberg, 1988). Her observations led her to believe that their open sexuality separated them from American adolescents who live in a country that does not support adolescent promiscuity. Her research and published writings implied that the less stress experienced by Samoan adolescents was biologically driven (Feinburg, 1988).

Derek Freeman criticized Mead's work. He stated that Mead was misled and even lied to by Samoan adolescents and women; he suggested that there were no differences between the development of Americans and Samoans.

* dfrances@yahoo.com; (317) 809-3421.
† leeunde@regent.edu; (757) 630-4442.
‡ ayrswas@mail.regent.edu; (757) 352-4000.
§ Tmoxley21@gmail.com; (757) 352-4000.

Regardless of Freeman's critiques of Mead's work, however, one thing is for sure; her research in Samoa shed light on the idea that culture influences personal attributes and characteristics (Choudhury, 2010; Feinberg, 1988; Freeman, 1983& Shankman, 2013).

A brief definition for the terms "culture" and "social" will be provided in this chapter. Slattery (2004) interprets culture as a way of life that is more noticeable when it stands out as different and not similar. No person stands separate from the influence of culture. People and culture go hand and hand. Setting the very tone of habit and decisions is the influence of culture. Determining what to eat, how to live, who to affiliate with and who to marry are all connected to a person's cultural setting. The difficulty here is that when a person begins to live in a culture unlike their own they are at risk of being socially unaccepted by the people in that culture (Slattery, 2004).

The term "social," on the other hand, is a term used to describe the interaction between two or more people. According to Vygotsky's theory, social interaction is the creative factor for a particular culture to develop (Berk, 2008). Social interaction is needed for younger generations to learn the norms and rules of that culture in order to survive. Learning and transmitting culture through social avenues happens in all cultures. Again, hence the hardship that may be experienced by children and adolescents who are forced to live in an unfamiliar culture.

Consider the experiences of adolescents who move from Mexico to the United States. These adolescents are oftentimes forced to learn a new language, change their style of dress, and learn the norms and rules of living that are unlike their own. Having to choose between leaving their old traditions behind and accepting the new are choices they often must make. However, this act of learning how to fit in could take years. Language acquisition, for instance, for ethnic minority children who are learning how to speak and write English as their second language, first language being Spanish, can take up to 34 months before they catch up to their peers (Goldberg, Paradis, & Crago, 2008).

Acculturation is defined as the personal change that happens to a person when they move from one culture to another; as a result of this change they begin to take on the attributes, characteristics, and personhood of their new culture (Murray et al., 2014). Now, acculturation has the potential for the development of risk factors; adolescents who find themselves an outcast from their peers because of the inability to fit in due to cultural factors (e.g., language) are at risk of depression (Lorenzo-Blanco, Unger, Baezconde-Garbanati, Ritt-Olson, & Soto, 2012).

Thereby, this is a chapter about the social and cultural issues present in adolescence. Specific focus is on how social and cultural factors interweave into adolescent development to create experience, shedding light on how these factors may contribute to youth engagement in socially deviant behaviors. As it turns out, culture and social settings influence adolescents' choices and behaviors. Before introducing this significant topic a few more terms need to be defined. First, collectivist cultures maintain that the group as a whole is the most important entity as opposed to the individual person; whereas individualistic cultures believe that the individual is the most important entity and strives to promote "self" and not "other" (Kanchier, 2007). Generally, and for purposes of this chapter, collectivist refers to Eastern and Asian cultures, while individualistic refers to European and American cultures (Kanchier, 2007). Two additional terms that need to be defined are: (1) Autonomy: A person gaining the ability to take self-initiative and regulate their own behaviors (Asakawa & Csikszentmihalyi, 2000); and (2) minority: As referred to in this chapter, means a person who is ethnically and racially different within their larger social context. Lastly, unless the research was directly focused on one particular population within the United States, all research referenced in this chapter took into account people of different cultures, races, and ethnicities.

The first part of this chapter explains how adolescence and culture interrelate and create experience. Next, the focus is on adolescent morality; this is defined as the understanding of what is right and wrong (Merriam-Webster, 2014). Following morality is a focus on the formation of adolescent self-identity. In addition, some of the factors that influence self-identity are explained such as self-esteem, acculturation, gender, and psychosocial characteristics. The next big focus is on the social development of adolescence. Social development impacts an adolescent's motivation and social skills and is impacted by an adolescent's social contexts: family, school, and neighborhood. Inevitably, this part of the chapter links social development with the formation of self-identity. Lastly, implications for justice involved youth is provided. As such, each part of this chapter interweaves special considerations for developmental impacts on adolescent involvement in delinquent or criminal behaviors.

Group formation and seeking out friendships are important to consider next. Adolescence is a crucial time for peer groups to form and friendships to be made, as they also help form an adolescent's self-identity. However, some adolescents find making friends difficult, which is itself a risk factor for negative interpersonal dynamics. The subject of interpersonal dynamics follows group formation. Within this subject there are three areas that are important to consider: peer pressure, peer rejection, and bullying. This chapter will focus on who are at most risk for these types of dynamics and the risk factors for developmental problems when they occur.

A case scenario, then, is used to describe the consequences of counselor negligence; followed by the ethical and legal obligations of such a case. Subsequently, provider consideration for when to provide a client with a referral, assess for suicide, and when to take extra precautions when diagnosing is explained. These areas are especially relevant to consider within a multicultural setting such as, where the counselor and client are culturally, racially, and/or ethnically different. In closing, this chapter ends with recommendations to counselors for how to offer competent counseling to minority clients.

The overall objective of this chapter is to provide readers with basic knowledge on social, cultural factors, and interpersonal issues with regards adolescence and justice involved youth. These factors or issues are important for counselors working with adolescents and preadolescents to understand, as they will impact the therapeutic relationship and process. After reading this chapter, readers will be able to:

- Identify cultural differences in adolescent development and how culture may impact adolescents' development and expression of moral reasoning.
- Describe the role of identity in adolescence and the affect of culture on the adolescent pursuit to self-identify. Additionally, readers will understand how self-esteem, materialism, acculturation, gender and psychosocial influences influence identity development.
- Understand the social development of adolescents, and its impact on self-identity.
- Demonstrate knowledge on the impact of friendships and group formation on adolescent development, and juvenile justice involvement by identifying interpersonal protective and risk factors and their influence on the adolescent.
- Demonstrate understanding of how social, developmental, and interpersonal factors impact adolescents' involvement in criminal and delinquent behaviors.
- Apply knowledge gained from this chapter to a case scenario.

CULTURE AND ADOLESCENT DEVELOPMENT

"Age is a convenient way to define adolescence. But it is only one characteristic that delineates this period of development. Age is often more appropriate for assessing and comparing biological changes (e.g., puberty), which are fairly universal, than the social transitions, which vary more with the socio-cultural environment" (World Health Organization (WHO), 2014, para 4). While most cultures recognize there is a transition time between childhood and adulthood they often do not agree with what to call this period of life or what ages fall within it (WHO, 2014). Consider, for example, these statistics: International Labor Organization, United Nations (UN) Secretariat, and the UN Educational Scientific and Cultural Organization label people between the ages of 15 – 24 "youth" (UN Instruments, Statistics); UN Habitat (Youth fund) use the word "youth" to describe people ages 15 – 32 (Agenda 21); UN Population Fund uses the word "youth" for ages 15 – 24; The United Nations Children's Fund (UNICEF): "adolescence" ages 10 – 19; The World Health Organization (WHO): "young people" ages 10 – 24 (UNFPA); The Convention on Rights of the Child: "child until 18" (UNICEF); and The African Youth Charter: "youth" ages 15 – 35 (African Union, 2006;United Nations, 2014). These statistics support the notion that culture does affect a person's perception of development and life. It also suggests that different cultures experience this period of development differently than other cultures, as the ages marking this period of life changes considerably from one country to the next.

Culture is created through the natural interaction between groups of people, based on their shared experiences. Furthermore, culture is related to environment, which contains the norms and societal rules. These cultures, therefore, teach people how to survive within specific social contexts (i.e., different cultures have different rules so that people can survive within them; Lopez, 2011; Massimini & Fave, 2000). Culture is a set of engrained values in a person, teaching them how to act and react and most importantly, how to socialize. Essentially, there are thousands of different cultures in the world (e.g., ethnic cultures, religious cultures, technology culture, adolescent culture, adult culture; Swatos, 1998). There are even cultures within cultures. For example, consider a Mexican immigrant family moving to a state in the Midwest region of the United States (Bennett, Chown, & Kang, 2005).

When considering the current cultures within the United States, there are unique distinctions that are particular to adolescents. For example, an adolescent in the United States may tend to highly value the latest video game, adhere to norms regarding hanging out at the mall for many hours, believe that love at first sight is essential to romantic relationships, or find it essential to adhere to the latest fashions and slang (Swatos, 1998). While other cultures (e.g., adult culture) may also express some of these same values, norms, beliefs, and expressions, they are not as common among other cultural groups. For example, if a middle-aged adult were to dawn a half shaven hairstyle, the likelihood of a negative response from peers, employers, family members and religious leaders may be met with much disapproval. Whereas, her adolescent counterpart may experience negative feedback, but may more than likely be seen as a brave, trend setting, or as a creative nonconformist. The adolescent who is adept at predicting reactions and socially navigating this dichotomy seem to fair better than those who are less skilled in anticipating other's reactions and dealing with them effectively. Adolescents are also known for their contrasting morals, pushing limits, trying new behaviors, and learning more about themselves through their experiences, which tend to differ from general societal norms, rules, manners, expectations, and role identity.

Moral Reasoning

Moral development begins to take shape in children as young as two (Brownell, 2013). They learn early from people around them that certain behaviors are right (e.g., sharing and being polite) and others are wrong (e.g., biting and kicking). However, culture has a way of defining morality. Adolescents from different cultures display evidence that moral behavior changes as culture changes (Carlo, Fabes, Laible, & Kupanoff, 1999). For instance, significant amounts of Asian and Mexican adolescent's moral behavior are socially focused and they may not feel pressured by a moral obligation to help others; instead they genuinely feel the need to engage in helping behaviors. On the other hand, White adolescents' moral behavior tend to be more about gaining approval (i.e., they are motivated to help in order to gain acceptance from their parents and peers) (Carlo et al., 1999). White, Carlo, Eisenberg, and Knight (1992) shed light on Brazilian adolescents' moral behavior. According to their research, Brazilian adolescents tend to help others because they feel empathy for them. While the aforementioned characteristics about adolescents from different backgrounds may be common in the literature, it is important for the provider to assess each adolescent on his/her own merit. That is, while some of the stereotypes about adolescents may be helpful and serve as a guide in characterizing and case conceptualizing adolescents, they should not serve as an iron clad rule of thumb.

Morality is learned through two parental avenues including modeling and discipline (as hypothesized by Carlo et al., 1999). As culture changes, parenting styles also change, resulting in a change in moral development and behavior (Ferguson, Hagaman, Maurer, Mathews, & Peng, 2013). Consider, for example, the industrialization and technological advancements of India. India is beginning to resemble the advancements of the United States and China in the said areas. Interesting, as India's culture changes, their parenting styles also change. Reportedly, their parenting styles are starting to reflect a "laissez-faire" parenting style with reduced pressure to conform to group standards and more inclined to be independently driven, much like their American and Chinese counterparts (Ferguson et al., 2013). Laissez-faire characterizes parents who are nonchalant in their parenting approach often allowing their children to have free-range over their choices, and provide very few restrictions (Bowers, 2014).

Because the focus of this chapter is on the period of adolescence, the stage of development that will be highlighted from Kohlberg's theory is the post conventional level—the fifth and sixth stage. This stage, especially, marks a time when adolescents are becoming increasingly aware of their social worlds (e.g., norms, standards, laws, rules) and are often presented with conflicting choices (Bae, 1999). For example, adolescents going through this stage struggle with whether or not they should lie or tell the truth, respect for self, respect for communities, and a desire to be honest are all important areas within this stage (Bae, 1999).

Despite Kohlberg tremendous influence in the area of moral development, his theory has been questioned for its current applicability with adolescents from different cultural backgrounds (Mulla & Krishnan, 2014). For this reason, Mulla and Kirshnan (2014) suggest models of moral development that are aligned with eastern thought as more appropriate for ethnic minorities. They studied the model of moral development referred to as "Karma-Yoga." Through questionnaires and surveys they tested the model of Karma-Yoga with adults residing in the Indian nation of Bhagawad Gita. According to their study's results, the model was more applicable to the people in this nation. They hypothesized that the reason for this is because the model takes into account Indian religious beliefs, such as karma and reincarnation. Indian religious beliefs influence the behavior of its inhabitants; therefore, the Karma-Yoga model of moral development is applicable to adolescents as well, as they too are embedded in this context (Mulla & Kirshnan, 2014).

Religious commitments do affect adolescent morality (Schnitker, Felke, Barrett, & Emmons, 2014). Longitudinal research shows that Christian adolescents abstain from dating and sexual encounters (e.g., masturbation, sexual partners) longer than adolescents who are not Christian (Pedersen, 2014). The greater the commitment to Christianity, for example, the lower the likelihood adolescents engaged in masturbation and early sexual experimentation (Pedersen, 2014). The difference in the sexual activity of non-Christians versus Christians was significant for 13 year old adolescents. Two hundred and ninety-six non-Christian and 45 Christian adolescents answered "yes" to making out and 178 non-Christian and 21 Christian adolescents reported being touched on their genitals, At the age of 16 years old and younger, 201 non-Christian adolescents and 5 Christian adolescents had their first experience with intercourse. At the age of 21 years, non-Christians reported having 5.7 sexual partners while Christians reported 1.8 sexual partners. The number of sexual partners increased to 11.1 for non-Christians and 4.2 for Christians by the time they were 28 years old (Pedersen, 2014).

In yet another study, surveys given to adolescents before and after a Christian camping trip found that those who converted over to Christianity reflected changes in their morality (Schnitker et al., 2014). This studies show the relevance of spirituality and religion in the lives of adolescents and providers should consider these issues while treating the needs of adolescents who are spiritually committed (Yukl, 2012).

Based on our general understanding of human development and the developmental process of moral reasoning, the juvenile justice system has developed a unique culture and set of beliefs itself. The primary presupposition from which the juvenile justice system was developed is that children and adolescents are different from adults and, therefore, they cannot be treated the same in the eyes of the law. Legally, children and adolescents are viewed differently from adults in that they are not of "full legal capacity" (OJJDP, 1999, p. 2), meaning they are not fully responsible for their actions. This is most obviously shown in the laws prohibiting children from activities such as voting, using alcohol, entering into contracts, for example. When considering the detention facilities housing adolescents, state agencies must protect these minors from their adult counterparts in adult facilities. In light of the protection need, the juvenile justice system exists separately from the adult justice system (McMillin, 2014).

Based on this premise of the difference between adults and adolescents, two further presuppositions have developed that have shaped the way in which the juvenile justice system operates and makes decision. These presuppositions are that adolescents have a diminished capacity and that juveniles (adolescents involved in the juvenile justice system) are malleable.

Juveniles and Diminished Capacity

Diminished capacity (or responsibility) is a legal defense that is used to argue that one cannot be held criminally responsible for his or her actions, as his or her mental functions were impaired. Legally, minors are prohibited from voting, entering into contracts, drinking alcohol, smoking, and participating in a variety of other activities because they are seen as not having the capacity to fully understand the impact of their decisions and behaviors. This same principle applies to infractions of the law in that adolescents are not viewed as fully responsible for their actions due to their lesser capacity to make decisions. This lesser capacity can be attributed to adolescents' ongoing cognitive, neurological (the decision making center in the brain (the prefrontal cortex), especially), and moral development.

Juveniles Are Malleable

One of the primary differences between adults and adolescents is the potential for change. Juveniles are developmentally in a period of transition. Legally, physically, emotionally, and mentally they are in a state of adjustment, moving from dependence to independence. Decisions made about adolescents in the juvenile justice system under the "best interest" principle take into consideration that, to a much greater degree than for adults, there remains the hope of change (McMillin, 2014). The malleability of juveniles is, in essence, a reflection of the process of self-discovery still occurring in adolescence.

Self-Identity

Self-identity refers to the makeup of a human being including their attributes, characteristics, ways of creating experience (Kroger, 1999; Lloyd, 2002). Self-identity begins with adolescents seeking out information from their social environments to inform them how to act and behave. Context, culture, and experience work as molding devices for these young people. For instance,

African American adolescent girls were found to be more accepting of larger body frames and challenges with obesity while Caucasian adolescent girls were more at risk for developing eating disorders (e.g., bulimia and anorexia; Mackey & Greca, 2008). Motivating these dimensions are the social ties adolescents have with peers and parents (Jones, 2014). Through these important relationships, adolescents receive verbal and nonverbal messages that inform them about who they are as individuals—these are crucial experiences for the development of identity. For instance, research by Mackey and Greca (2008) examined the risk factors for the development of eating disorders. They found that young girls were motivated to change the way they ate based simply on their friends' eating patterns. Perception was crucial here as adolescent girls were aligning their consumption of food intake with their idea of what was a "normal" amount of food to eat based on their friends' consumption. Hunger level was irrelevant and peer perceptions seemed to be at the forefront.

Adolescents also strive to fit in by giving into the pressure to act aggressively (i.e., intention to hurt another person). Social pressure is the number one predictor that adolescents will engage in aggressive behaviors (Yavuzer, Karatas, Civilidag, & Gundogu, 2014). The need to fit in and to identify with their peers becomes the overriding factor for their behavior (Yavuzer et al., 2014). As an example, Yavuzer et al, 2014 studied the notion of automatic thoughts. Automatic thoughts, defined as private conversations a person has with themselves that focuses on their past, present, and future, also precede adolescent aggressive behaviors (Yavuzer et al., 2014). An automatic thought could resemble the following: "She should not treat me that way" or "I deserve to sit at that desk." Social pressure and automatic thoughts, therefore, accounted for significant levels of aggression (measured by the Aggression Questionnaire (AQ); created by Buss & Perry and revised by Buss & Warren, 2000) in both boys (44.6%) and girls (27.6%) (Yavuzer et al., 2014). There are common diagnoses that are seen in delinquent adolescents. Two main categories of justice-involved adolescents (Crossover youth and antisocial/aggressive youth) are described here. It is important to remember that these categories are not exclusive of each other, in that adolescents may be able to fall into multiple categories. However, this chapter presents the categories separately in the next three sections.

Crossover Youth

The first category, crossover youth, refers to adolescents who have experienced maltreatment and engaged in delinquent behaviors (Herz et al, 2010). These are adolescents who are often dually involved with child welfare services and the court system. They present a distinctive problem due to the many systems and organizations involved in their lives. For example an adolescent may have child services workers, probation officers, attorneys, biological parents, stepparents, foster parents, volunteer advocates, judges, case managers, and a therapist involved in his or her case. Furthermore, the adolescents' history of maltreatment adds an important trauma component to the circumstances and ensuing treatment needs.

Crossover youth usually have both dependency concerns (e.g., needing adult supervision, financial support, guidance, etc.) and delinquency involvement (e.g., legal concerns, detainment, treatment compliance, etc.) and are often caught between them. This means that an adolescent may be simultaneously involved with both probation and child welfare services as a result of parental acts of abuse and/or neglect. Research indicates that there is a connection between delinquency and histories of maltreatment (Herz et al., 2010; Ryan & Testa, 2004; Ryan, Williams, & Courtney, 2013). One study shows that maltreated adolescents have 47% higher delinquency rates as compared to their peers from the general population (Ryan & Testa, 2004). Not surprisingly, crossover youth are also at a greater risk for substance abuse and mental health problems than adolescents without a history of maltreatment (Herz et al., 2010). As such, crossover youth often present with a wide variety of disorders and diagnoses.

Antisocial Adolescents

Another group that present as challenges to community safety is that of the antisocial adolescent. Antisocial adolescents generally present with disruptive behavior disorders (conduct disorder, oppositional defiant disorder, intermittent explosive disorder etc.) and a greater association with violent street gangs (Sanders, 2012). They often present more aggressive and angry in their counseling sessions. Additionally, they have been shown to have a greater prevalence of suicidal ideation (Ruchkin, Schwab-Stone, Koposov, Vermeiren, & King, 2003; Thompson, Kingree, & Ho, 2006). Interpersonal callousness and antisocial traits are also frequently associated with this category of adolescents.

Research has shown a frequent occurrence of comorbidity with attention deficit hyperactivity disorder (AD/HD), conduct disorder (CD), and oppositional defiant disorder (ODD; Chen et al., 2013). Because several of the symptoms, of these disorders can appear very similar to one another, and many of these adolescents have been diagnosed with a wide range of behavioral health disorders. Diagnostic confusion can further reign when the symptoms are interpreted as being the result of mood disorders and not simply disruptive behavior. Consequently, these types of adolescents have been strongly associated with a greater prevalence for mood disorders (Chen et al., 2013).

When examining the risk of delinquency persisting into adulthood, researchers have noted specific symptoms that seem to pose a greater risk of ongoing delinquency. For example, adolescents who demonstrate conduct disorder and particularly interpersonal callousness symptoms are more likely to develop antisocial personality disorder and continued criminal activity as adults (Byrd, Loeber, & Pardini, 2011). However, adolescents who demonstrate primarily ADHD and/or ODD symptoms are more likely discontinue their antisocial behavior as they age.

Erik Erikson offered a slightly different perspective on self-identity. He theorized that adolescents arrive at the fifth stage of development, identity versus identity confusion (Lloyd, 2002). At this stage, identity formation begins with a time of crisis in which adolescents try to decide who they are as individuals. The core of Erikson's theory is individualization, characterized by a desire to establish a distinct, unique self (Berman, You, Schwartz, Teo, & Mochizuki, 2011; Cherry, 2014; Lloyd, 2002). Erikson's model of development, however, has been scrutinized for its current applicability to adolescent development and applicability for ethnic minority adolescents (Berman et al., 2011; Jones, 2014; O'Grady, 2006; Rotheram-Borus, 1989). Jones (2014) highlights the differences in current times, as opposed to 60 years ago when the Erikson model was first developed and normed. For example, Berman et al, 2011 and Brand, 2004, when studying Asian cultures, found that Erikson's model is focused on individuation and separating oneself from another. However, the emphasis placed on being independent and self-focused is highly aligned with European thought and lifestyle (Berman et al., 2011; Brand, 2004) more so than Asian lifestyle. Erikson's model, according to the said study, undermines the importance of family and cohesion seen in Asian cultures (Brand, 2004; Sok & Yun, 2011).

Building upon Erikson's theory of self-identity, Marcia, 1966, 1993 and Lloyd, 2002, they suggested there are four "statuses" that may be adopted by adolescents in this stage: "identity confused, foreclosed, moratorium, and identity achieved." Adolescents reach one of the four stages based on whether or not they have a firm understanding and commitment to their beliefs and whether or not they have engaged a developmental crisis (Lloyd, 2002). For example, in studying the impact of crisis in adolescents, Lloyd, 2002 suggested that those adolescents who are confused in their self-identify may be challenged by the idea that they have to choose one belief over another. The foreclosed adolescent, on the other hand, has some commitments to their beliefs but only out of the pressure from others. For example, they oftentimes adopt the values and beliefs of their parents. For those adolescents in the moratorium stage, or the active crisis stage tend to adopt a set of principles that they do not feel connected to. This leads them into a state of panic (Lloyd, 2002). Nonetheless, this stage is healthy and adolescents will go in and out of this stage during their course of development because it offers them a way to test out new beliefs and values. Identity achievement is the endpoint. These adolescents have a core set of beliefs, norms, and values (Lloyd, 2002). Marcia believed there was an ending point to the formation of identity. Erikson, however, disagreed. He believed that identity was always developing.

In the case of minority adolescents, their self-identity depends on the importance they place on their race and ethnicity. Charmaraman & Grossman (2010) offer that an adolescent's centrality (level of importance placed on race and ethnic identity) is a significant part of their identity. As follows, when an adolescent has a propensity towards high centrality, they also have high internal pride. Consequently, African-American adolescents were found to have the highest centrality while biracial and Caucasian adolescents had the lowest (Charmaraman & Grossman, 2010). The implications to these findings suggest that minority adolescents (excluding biracial) view themselves as distinctly different and can be a source of esteem. Conversely, Charmaraman and Grossman (2010) found Caucasian and biracial adolescents have difficulty seeing themselves as distinct races and may resort to "color blindness" and present with a low sense of centrality in which racial and ethnic identity is not a big part of their personal identity (Charamaraman & Grossman, 2010).

Self-Esteem and the Value of Materialism

Chaplin, Hill, and John (2014) link self-esteem with self-identity formation in adolescence. Their research indicates that adolescents seek out ways to enhance their self-esteem in order to build their self-identities. One way adolescents have been found to accomplish this is through materialism. Essentially, because adolescents are motivated by social stimuli (reflected in later sections) they try to enhance the way others perceive them by gaining materialistic items. However, this becomes difficult when adolescents live in poverty or are limited by a low socioeconomic status.

Chaplin et al. (2014) studied the value of materialism in both impoverished and affluent adolescents. They created two groups: Impoverished (guardian income $25,688—below national median income) adolescents and affluent (guardian income $96,080 to $187,574) adolescents, all between the ages of eight – 10 years old (Chaplin et al., 2014; U.S. Bureau of the Census 2010). Out of the two groups, each person individually made their own collage out of a pool of 100 pictures. The results showed that impoverished adolescents had more materialistic pictures (e.g., car, house, money) and affluent adolescents had more relationship pictures (e.g., adult and child sitting closely, child playing with a dog) (Chaplin et al., 2014). The study implied materialism is more important to impoverished adolescents at a higher rate than affluent adolescents. They hypothesized the reasons for this difference was because affluent adolescents have at their "disposal" the items they need and thus do not "fantasize" about these items; whereas impoverished adolescents are in a constant state of deprivation so they fantasize about those things they do not have.

Clash of Cultures

"Clash of cultures"—or "meme competition" (Massimini & Fave, 2000) defines what happens when two or more different cultures come together (Charamaraman & Grossman, 2010). A common term used to describe "clash of cultures" and "meme competition" is acculturation (i.e., a person's ability to learn the rules and customs of their new culture). Moreover, acculturation is the "nonnormative" process of dealing with the challenges of life (Terzini-Hollar, 2008). The issue with immigrant adolescents is that oftentimes acculturation is difficult and their adjustment to the new culture becomes stressful and can create developmental challenges (e.g., difficulty forming relationships, identity confusion) (Terzini-Hollar, 2008; Rajiva, 2006). Arnett (2002) and Berman et al. (2011) suggests identity confusion is the result of living within two different cultures with "competing" belief systems. Suggesting that rather than trying to be independent, these adolescents are just try to fit in—which they do by trying to become "bicultural" (i.e., integrating their traditional culture and their embedded culture) (Berman et al., 2011).

Rajiva (2006) was interested in understanding the acculturation experience of Asian adolescents. Her research specifically looked at the development of Asian adolescent girls in Western society. She found that Asian adolescents had difficulty feeling a sense of belonging from the dominant culture (e.g., White culture). In addition, Asian adolescents stated in a survey that they were frustrated with their parents for not allowing them to hang out with their White peers or practice White cultural norms (e.g., dating) (Rajiva, 2006) because their parents restricted them to only hanging out with Asian peers. Consequently, these adolescents felt a sense of exclusion from their embedded culture (e.g., American culture) and their traditional culture (Asian culture). Essentially, many of them grew up feeling disconnected and confused (i.e., unable to build a secure self-identity) because they wanted to be a part of the American culture and felt a closer connection to it than to their traditional culture, as they often were first generation Americans who had never experienced their traditional culture within its actual context (Rajiva, 2006). Consequently, they feel like they are in a constant struggle between two cultures. Here is one Vietnamese girls' account of this experience:

> "I just dyed my hair and my mom got all upset. My friends called me white at first when I was a brunette. I notice that appearance matters to ethnicity a lot. If you have long black hair, white skin, and short then you're fine. I cut my hair short like the little boyish look and my mom went crazy on me. She said you're not my daughter, you're like my son. I said, so! You want to do what makes you feel happy or comfortable but they put you in this little ethnicity box. Especially here (in Westminster). Going to church you wear ao dai (traditional Vietnamese dress). I'm not rebelling but I don't want to be another Asian girl in an American crowd. I want to be myself. I'm not going against my parents or tradition. I want to make my own morals and traditions and it makes me happy. It's not bad. I'm not doing drugs or tattooing myself. It makes me happy to have medium hair and to dye it."(Vo-Jutabha, 2005, p. 28).

Clearly, for some immigrant adolescents, acculturation can be a difficult process, as they have to learn the language, culture, dress, style, etiquette, rules, mannerisms, and ways of behaving of the dominant culture all while trying to fit in and make friends—a definite struggle for some. Other dynamics that tend to cause distress for adolescents are gender and psychosocial influences (e.g., parental restrictions, academic success, and puberty).

Gender and Psychosocial Influences

Adolescent girls are described as “interdependent,” with a propensity towards emotional and social stimuli whereas, adolescent boys are more oriented towards action and independence (Charmaraman & Grossman, 2010; Cross & Madson, 1997). Parents may be the context variable that influences girls and boys to differentiate the way they do, as research shows that parenting styles change depending on the gender of the child (Charmaraman & Grossman, 2010). For instance, parents regularly place more restrictions on girls than boys (e.g., girls have an earlier curfew). Additionally, girls are often treated fragilely (e.g., not allowed to play sports) and encouraged to take on gender specific roles (e.g., cleaning). As related to culture, ethnic minority (e.g., Latino) adolescent girls are expected to keep the family traditions and norms, whereas boys are given more freedom to gain autonomy (e.g., by seeking education and career status) in the world (Charmaraman & Grossman, 2010). In surveys between girls and boys of ethnic and racial minority status, girls reported more centrality than boys (i.e., family traditions, norms, race, and ethnicity more important to girls). However, only boys’ centrality related to school achievement (i.e., higher centrality equaled higher achievement) (Charmaraman & Grossman, 2010). Charmaraman and Grossman (2010) state the reason for the difference in centrality rates for boys and girls are again due in part because of environmental influences (e.g., parents, teachers, society). Girls are encouraged to keep their families’ traditions while boys are encouraged to seek autonomy through education and vocation. Interesting, this continues even through young adulthood, where girls and boys are encouraged to desire “gender” specific careers (e.g., girl to be a nurse; boy to be an engineer) (Zajko, 2007).

Girls and boys are also encouraged differently in school. Girls are encouraged to do well in language and writing and boys are encouraged to do well in math and science. Research in this area, furthermore, finds that when children and adolescents are encouraged to do well in certain areas and not others, it is reflected in their perceived ability to succeed in those areas and in their performance (e.g., girls who were encouraged to do well in language and not math responded in a survey that they were bad at math, good at language, and then performed accordingly). However, when the stereotype was reversed (i.e., girls believed they were good at math) performance continued to run parallel (i.e., girls outscored males in math achievement) (Steffens & Jelenec, 2011).

Finally, in the case of normal development, girls and boys alike will go through physical changes related to hormonal shifts (puberty). Adolescents in countries, such as Iran and Turkey, experience puberty differently than many American adolescents do (Golchin, Hamzehgardeshi, Fakhri, & Hamzehgardeshi, 2012). Golchin et al. (2012) provides an explanation for why this is so. In speaking for the country of Iran, these researchers state that there are "cultural restrictions" in place that do not allow for sexual education. Because of this restriction, adolescent girls do not receive the education concerning what to expect for this period of development. As a result, Iranian and Turkish girls, for instance, who get their period, are at times scared to admit it to their peers or parents for fear of rejection or ridicule. In addition, at times these young girls feel their period is evidence of a disease or sickness (Golchin et al., 2012; Ozdemir, Nazik, & Pasinlioglu, 2010).

Ozdemir et al. (2010) studied the experience of menarche in Turkish girls. Their study consisted of a sample of 191 Turkish girls. Out of the 191 participants, a little over half, 101, thought of puberty as a natural phase, while the remaining 90 reported it being the worst experience they had ever had. Ekerbicer et al. (2007) confirm that the experience of menarche in the country of Turkey is regarded as "taboo" and there is lack of systems in schools (e.g., sanitary facilities) that support this experience. A question arises as a result of the findings from the research by Ozdemir et al. (2010): How, despite the countries overall lack of education around sexual issues (Ekerbicer, Celik, Kiran, & Kiran, 2007), did over half the girls report the experience as natural and normal? Beyond this chapter's focus, but highlighting a research need, is research comparing the healthcare forums and parenting styles in adolescents who believe menarche to be natural versus terrible.

Muslim adolescent girls experience complete separation from their communities during times of their menarche, as they are not allowed to attend mosque during these times and report feeling ashamed and inadequate as a response to physical changes brought on by puberty Golchin et al., 2012). Muslims are accounted for in all parts of the world but are overrepresented in Indonesia (Ipenburg, 2012). The lack of education and acceptance of this time period may be a direct cause of the growing rate of anemia found present in adolescents in Indonesia (Sockarjo et al., 2001).

An important population to consider when discussing developmental, cultural, and social influences in adolescence, is justice involved juveniles, as culture and relationships heavily influence a youth's engagement in delinquent and criminal behavior. Over the years several different theories have emerged on the development of antisocial and delinquent behaviors. Theorists focus primarily on developmental or environmental factors as greatest contributors (Tremblay, 2000), yet consideration of either should not exclude the other.

Developmental theorists place greater importance on the makeup of the individual than on the environmental factors that influence the adolescent. In regards to delinquency, developmental theorists point to studies that show a great increase in delinquent and aggressive behavior in children when they reach adolescence. The rapid increase in delinquent behavior, which begins at adolescence and then sees an equally rapid decrease, is called the age-crime curve. Studies have found that, as children age, they become more physically aggressive (Tremblay, 2000). Therefore, age is seen as a major factor in the development of aggressive behavior. Beauchaine, Hinshaw, & Pang (2010) studied disruptive behaviors disorders and state that:

> Delinquent boys usually traverse a developmental pathway that begins with severe hyperactive /impulsive behaviors as early as toddlerhood, followed by ODD (oppositional defiant disorder) in preschool, early-onset CD (conduct disorder) in elementary school, substance use disorders (SUDs) in adolescence, and antisocial personality in adulthood (p. 328)

Byrd, Loeber & Pardini (2011) took this research a step further and found that interpersonal callousness, in particular, was the primary indicator of disruptive behavior disorders that would persist into adulthood antisocial behavior. Additionally, the comorbidity of conduct disorder and mood disorders have also been connected to an increase in delinquent behavior (Chen et al., 2013). Gender differences have been examined in relation to the development of delinquency as well (Walters, 2014). In this way, developmental theories focus more specifically on the qualities that make up the individual. However, environment and relationships play an important role in adolescent development, and their development of antisocial, delinquent, and criminal behaviors.

ADOLESCENT SOCIAL DEVELOPMENT

Lev Vygotsky, a leading theorist in the field of adolescent social development, believed adolescents must be studied within their social contexts (e.g., school environment; Higa & Brandon, 2000). Within the school environment, for example, friends are essential; in fact, they have the power to influence both positive and negative development. Positive social development characterizes adolescents who have a strong sense of personal identity and problem solving skills. Additionally, these adolescents show evidence of extensive skill in developing and maintaining social ties (Thomas & Joseph, 2013; WHO, 2008).

Friendships provide a sense of belonging. The sense of belonging raises self-esteem and decreases the chances of depression (Adams & Cantin, 2013). However, when adolescents lack friendships, the outcome is a feeling of rejection (Kim-Gervey, 2008). Rejection, then, can lead to depression (Kim-Gervey, 2008; Satomi, Ogawa, & Wilson, 2002). As with the importance of friendships, research also supports the notion that adolescents are in need of positive social influences from their family and teachers as well (Mayer, Garofalo, & Makadon, 2014; Oberle, Schonert-Reichl, & Zumbo, 2011). These influences have the potential to lead to an adolescent feeling inspired and encouraged to achieve in school and experience self-growth.

Developmental systems theory suggests a "bidirectional" relationship between individuals and their environments (Theokas et al., 2005); maintaining that young people have a hand in their own development when they align their strengths with environmental resources (Oberle et al., 2011). When adolescents are connected to these systems (home and school) in a positive way, their developmental trajectory runs parallel in a positive way. A connection to these systems requires the influence of peers and adults as they make the connection possible. However, the connection must be one of support and comfort in order for healthy development to be the outcome. When support and comfort are present, adolescents who are highly connected to school have more confidence, school success, and overall perseverance. In addition, adolescents who are connected to school and to their communities (e.g., neighborhood) are less victimized (e.g., bullied) and are less likely to become depressed (Lesters, Waters, & Cross, 2013; Turner, Reynolds, Lee, Subasic, & Bromhead, 2014).

Whether or not an adolescent is able to form a positive social identity depends on their ability to enter a peer group, relate to their peers, and fit in to the norms and culture in which they live. Finally, the formation of an adolescent's social identity depends on their family context, social motivation and skill level, their participation in social interactions, and their school and neighborhood influences (Chen & Farruggia, 2002; Massimini & Fave, 2000; Oberle et al., 2011; Vo-Jutabha, 2005; Yoo, 2009).

Impact of Environment and Justice Involved Youth

Unlike developmental theorists, Environmental theorists, look more at the social context and systems that interact with and surround the adolescent. These theorists point to the powerful impact that families, peers, and neighborhoods can have on development (Tremblay, 2000) as evidence that the environment plays the primary role in shaping behavior. Deviant behavior, in particular, has been linked to social contexts in several studies (Jennings, Maldonado-Molina, Reingle, & Komro, 2011). An example of one environmental theory is called Social Disorganization Theory. This theory "emphasizes the importance of the ability of a community's residents to realize shared goals and values and regulate the conduct of its citizens" (Jennings et al., 2011, p. 393). Adolescents residing in communities that are characterized by higher crime rates and greater residential instability are at a far greater risk of developing delinquent behavior than their peers in other areas of town. Moreover, the impact of deviant peers on other adolescents has long been studied and shown to have negative effects on treatment outcomes and future offending behavior (Dodge, Dishion, & Lansford, 2006; Sanders, 2012). Parenting techniques and familial disruption have also been shown to have a great impact on a child's propensity to develop aggressive and delinquent behaviors (Cashmore, 2011; Krinsky, 2010; Piquero, Farrington, Welsh, Tremblay, & Jennings, 2009; Walters, 2014). Research has shown how aggression in parents directly impacts the development of externalizing, disruptive behaviors in their children (Hops, Davis, Leeves, & Sheeber, 2003).

Differing Pathways

Taking a different route, some theorists have begun concentrating on what they consider differing pathways to developing offending and delinquent behavior. These theorists place less emphasis on finding the cause and more on identifying the paths and factors that can play important roles in promoting such behavior (Walters, 2014). One of the dangers of looking at these pathways, however, is to begin following a one-size-fits-all approach to every adolescent. Every adolescent is unique with his or her own story that deserves attention. Notwithstanding, these pathways can help create a framework that allows providers to better conceptualize the problems and life events with which the adolescent presents in counseling sessions.

One pathway to delinquent behavior that has been extensively examined is the trauma pathway. We have already discussed crossover youths in this chapter. Studies have shown the connection between child maltreatment and neglect and aggressive/disruptive behavior (Krinsky, 2010; Ryan & Testa, 2004; Ryan, Williams & Courtney, 2013). This pathway views adolescent aggressive behavior as primarily reactions to previous maltreatment. In a study that examined externalizing behaviors across generational lines, researchers found that "adolescents who were exposed to greater levels of parental hostility were more likely to display aggressive behavioral styles as adolescents, with this behavioral style predicting the nature of their interactions with their own children" (Hops et al., 2003, p. 167). In short, adolescents who have developed delinquent behaviors through the trauma pathway are victims of direct (to the adolescents specifically) or indirect (observed, anticipated, or threatened) abuse or neglect. These adolescents have unresolved histories of trauma that are fueling their delinquent behaviors. From this perspective, helping an adolescent alter his or her aggressive behavior must, in some way, address the earlier trauma. Research indicates that there is a connection between delinquency and histories of maltreatment (Herz et al., 2010; Ryan & Testa, 2004; Ryan, Williams, & Courtney, 2013). One study shows that maltreated adolescents have 47% higher delinquency rates as compared to their peers from the general population (Ryan & Testa, 2004). More specific statistics are difficult to find due factors such as the intervention of various agencies, managing ethical compliance to confidentiality, information sharing between them all, and working with the same individual client.

Another pathway to delinquent behavior focuses predominantly on the familial and environmental factors. Adolescents from this pathway have been powerfully influenced by the context around them. Researchers have identified that parental behavior and deviant peer association have been closely linked to antisocial adolescent behavior (Deutsch, Crockett, Wolff, & Russell, 2012). Parenting styles that have less parental control (or influence that results in the adolescent restraining their behaviors, following directives, or heeding parental guidance) over the adolescent are directly correlated with an increase in delinquency rates and affiliations with delinquent peers. One study from

2012 showed that "maternal support was related to less association with deviant peers for African American and European American adolescents, which in turn predicted lower involvement in delinquent behaviors" (Deutsch et al., 2012, p. 1089). This means that the adolescents whose mothers were more involved in their lives were less likely to engage in delinquent behavior than their peers with more distant mothers. Furthermore, neighborhood factors such as crime rates, socioeconomic status, and neighborhood cohesion have also been shown to greatly affect delinquency rates (Jennings et al, 2011).

In other words, adolescent delinquency is closely related to contextual, environmental, and familial factors. Adolescents are influenced by the world around them. For the provider working with adolescents who have developed delinquent behaviors through this pathway, it is paramount to be able to identify and address the external factors that influence the adolescent towards delinquency.

The Resiliency Theory (RT) is a specific derivation of the impact of trauma studies have had on working with juvenile populations. This theory combines the family pathways toward delinquency with environmental pathways to understand and treat delinquent adolescents. It uses a positive psychology outlook and, as such, is more concerned with adolescent strengths rather than deficits. This RT theory looks at what makes it possible for adolescents to overcome the difficult settings in which they are raised by addressing the adolescents' assets (internal positive factors such as intelligence, temperament, impulse control) and resources (external positive factors such as effective schools, family supports, activities and hobbies). From this perspective it is important to focus on the strengths of the adolescent and the protective factors (like family involvement, social skills, competency, and community involvement) from which to build more individualized treatment plans and interventions (Fergus and Zimmerman, 2005) and life in general.

Essentially, theories on the development of aggressive and delinquent behavior have followed the same nature-nurture debate as in other aspects of psychology and continue to change as studies further shape our understanding of human behavior. Through last 30 years, longitudinal studies and research have shown us some of the important factors and pathways to delinquency. From these it is evident that factors associated with the adolescent's development (physical), experience (daily life), biology (disease or mental health challenges), environment (neighborhood safety), social (peer associations), and familial (support, supervision) all play a part and must be assessed and addressed in order to effectively treat justice-involved adolescents.

Social Identity

Where do I fit in? It is a common question that typifies the period between adolescence and adulthood. In other words, adolescents find themselves in a precarious position pertaining to where they fit in with others. They are not children that need constant supervision and direction, yet they are generally inexperienced with the world around them. At the same time, they do not have the financial independence as do adults. Adolescents continue to need guidance and are increasing in their strides toward full adult autonomy. Concomitantly, they engage in their own personal quests to discover their individuality, specialness, and efficacy within their families, friends, school, and community. This is evidenced in adolescents who discover their athletic skills, intellectual prowess, join clubs, and establish elaborate social events within the real and virtual worlds through their various social interaction means (technical and otherwise).

Adolescents are drawn to similarity (Bae, 1999; Garrett & McCoy, 2007; Kim-Gervey, 2008; Sentse et al., 2013; Zajko, 2008). They want to be connected to the people, places, and things they want to be. Whatever group they identify with, becomes linked to them—in effect indicating that "I represent this" (Garrett and McCoy, 2007; Mackey & Greca, 2008). Much like self-identity an adolescent's social identity is still forming in adolescents (Swatos, 1998). As a consequence, adolescents become overly concerned about what others think of them, entering the stage of self-criticism (Chaplin et al., 2014). From what to wear to how to speak, adolescents look for any opportunity to fit in with their peers, appear better than the norm (i.e., desire high social status), and take on the role of adults by engaging in risky behaviors (e.g., unprotected sex, drug use) (Friedlander, Connolly, Pepler, & Craig, 2007). In addition, adolescents' low impulse control at this stage of development is a risk factor for being engaged in illegal (e.g., stealing) and deadly (e.g., speed racing) behaviors (Chaplin et al., 2014; Zajko, 2007). However, when an adolescent's family context is supportive (e.g., no in-home domestic violence, parents are available) the lower the likelihood (i.e., risk factor) that they will participate in risky behaviors (e.g., unprotected sex) (Chen & Farruggia, 2002; Friedlander et al., 2007).

FRIENDSHIPS AND GROUP FORMATIONS

The core of healthy development is friendships (Oberle et al., 2011). It is interesting to think about the fact that for many centuries people have understood the following adage to be true: "Two people are better off than one, for they can help each other succeed" (Ecclesiastes 4:9, New Living Translation). Friendships, inevitably, have been found to influence development because they are a source of support, care, and a sense of belonging. They are also a source of protection; with the more friends one has the less likely they are to be victimized—also known as the "friendship protection hypothesis" (Sentse et al., 2013, p. 230).

In addition to the protective factor of friendships, they also have the potential to increase and sustain a sense of satisfaction with life. Even the perception that an interpersonal relationship is healthy, can have a positive effect on an adolescent's experience of life (Sentse et al., 2013; Oberle et al., 2011). However, adolescents who have difficulties in forming friendships are at risk for having low self-esteem, school achievement difficulties, suicidal ideation, and may experience bullying (Sentse et al., 2013). Oftentimes victims stand alone as whole groups of their peers will form and attack them verbally and physically. An adolescent who does not have friends is at great developmental risk because the possibility for this youth to gain entrance into a peer group becomes unlikely, as adolescents are less likely to allow someone into their peer groups if the person is being victimized (Sentse et al., 2013).

"Collective self-esteem" is the sense of pride that a person feels as a result of their peer groups' race and ethnicity (Charmaraman & Grossman, 2013). Furthermore, collective self-esteem has been found to have a positive influence on youth who identify as being a part of diverse races (e.g., Mexican, Chinese, Black). Collective self-esteem also predicts self-esteem among these young people and because of such, it is important to enhance self-esteem in adolescents (Charmaraman & Grossman, 2013).

Just like friendship, "peer crowds" form based on similarities. Peer crowds form based on reputable attributes. Peer crowds are bigger in size and members may or may not hang out with each other. Peer crowds include: (1) Popular, Brains (smart); (2) Burnouts (troublemakers); (3) Jocks (sports enthusiast); (4) Alternatives (rebels); (5) Average (no identified group); (6) Goths; and (7) Punks (Besic, 2011; Brown, 1990; La Greca and Prinstein, 1999; Mackey & Greca, 2008, p. 1098). Identification with any one peer group is up to adolescents. Choosing what crowd they want to be a part of is, from the very outset of their adolescent years, a primary goal. However, oftentimes groups such as the "Populars" is not self-chosen but instead assigned to people based on their attributes and overall style of appearance (Besic, 2011). On the other hand, people in such groups as Goths or Punks must be intentional with their involvement in these groups, as they have to outwardly look the part (e.g., spiking their hair, wearing fake eye lashes) (Besic, 2011). These crowds afford young people the sense of belonging and fitting in that they need during this stage of development (Kobus, 2003; Mackey & Greca, 2008; Prinstein & La Greca, 2002; Sussman et al., 1990). They also, nonetheless, can be a source of risk.

Goths, Punks, Synths (black clothing, interest in technology), and Aesthetics (painted face, music and art driven) are listed under the subtitle "Radicals" (Besic, 2011). These types of peer crowds standout because their appearances are "shocking" and socially unaccepted (e.g., all black clothing, boys with painted nails, dreadlocks). Besic and Kerr (2009) set out to determine whether adolescents in the Radical group were more or less reserved socially than other adolescent peer crowds. They compared Radical group members to two groups: Independents (no self-identified group affiliation) and Non-Radicals. Non-radical members included groups such as "Jocks," "Vegans," "Skaters," "Ravers," "Snobs," "Sports," "Role-Players," "Teenyboppers," "Feminists," "Hip-Hoppers," and "Poppers" (Besic & Kerr, 2009). Their results revealed that Radical group members are more reserved, shy, depressed, and have lower self-esteem than members in the other two groups (Besic & Kerr, 2009).

Compared to "Jocks" or "Nerds," adolescents who make up the "Goth" or "Punk" groups (i.e., Radicals) are at great risk for attempting suicide and engaging in self-harm (e.g., cutting) (Young, Sproeber, Grosschwitz, Preiss, & Plener, 2014). Adolescents self-identifying as "Jock" have higher self-esteem and are 80% less likely to attempt suicide than members in the "Alternative" (Goth, Punk) groups (Young et al., 2014). Jocks and Preps are at the top of the pecking order when it comes to peer group social ranking (Brady, 2004). Surveys revealed that adolescents unanimously agreed, Jocks and Preps are the most important people in school. "Nerds," "Dirts" "Stoners" and also "Goths," on the other hand, are at the bottom of the social scale. Outcast because of their outward appearance, these individuals are often hated by their peers (Brady, 2004).

There is a "selection" and "influence" process that goes into group formation. The selection process concerns the process of choosing friends and the influence process is how behaviors of individual members are influenced via the group. Additionally, due to their lack of social skills, even victimized adolescents are more likely to select other victimized adolescents to befriend. This is referred to as "default selection" (Mackey & Greca, 2008; Sijtsema, Lindenberg, & Veenstra, 2010; Sentse et al., 2013). This scenario becomes a risk factor because, when youth form groups based on their reality of victimization, victimization tends to increase not decrease (Sentse et al., 2013).

Choosing friends is also a protective factor. Friendships offer adolescents support and a sense of belonging, reducing their risk factors for depression and bullying (Mackey & Greca, 2008; Turner et al., 2014). Taking the already mentioned peer group affiliations, adolescents have a choice in which group they become a member of. Oftentimes, they choose the group as much as the group chooses them (Mackey & Greca, 2008). Two great selection motivators for young people include choosing friends based on similar race and similar ethnic background (Garrett & McCoy, 2007).

Peer Pressure

An adolescent's social network has the ability to "shape, train, and reinforce (their) behaviors" that are against social standards (Friedlander et al., 2007, p. 823). Again, adolescents' desire to imitate adulthood and adult norms pressures them to begin partaking in adult-like behaviors (e.g., sex, dating) (Friedlander et al., 2007). Peer pressure can feel like a demand to behave in uncomfortable ways or against a person's morals and values (e.g., drug use). Peer groups oftentimes hold to the belief that the behaviors they take part in are acceptable and "just a part of being young" (e.g., drunkenness). Their beliefs, furthermore, are considered to be a kind of "dogma" or "stigmatizing deviance" that pressures young people to act in ways that are not only demoralizing (e.g., lying) but also dangerous (e.g., sexually transmitted diseases) (Crenshaw & Markley, 2010, p. 1). Acting out in these ways becomes the social norm, which means that those who do not partake in the acts are seen as outsiders to the "faith" of adolescent culture (Crenshaw & Mackey, 2010). One example: Friedlander et al. (2007) found that the dating behavior in adolescents' was directly linked to the dating behavior of all members of that group. In fact, dating has been found to originate out of peer group pressure; as such, it is a subtle "influence" of the daily interaction with their peer group members that motivate adolescents' behavior to conform and imitate the norm (Crenshaw & Mackley, 2010; Friedlander et al., 2007).

Rejection is a form of discrimination and incredibly insidious as it undermines the very need for closeness and support that young people need.

Developmental problems are highly likely when a young person experiences or even perceives rejection. The idea of perception is significant here, as even just the perception of rejection can create issues (Kim-Gervey, 2008). Depression (Liu, 2014), anxiety (Rudolph, 2014), self-harm (McMahon, Reulbach, Keeley, Perry, & Arensman, 2010), and suicide (Campos, Besser, & Blatt, 2013) are all risk factors when an adolescent is rejected. The reason these risk factors are significant is that the adolescent receives information about themselves through feedback from their peers and parents. If the feedback is mostly negative, then the adolescent is more likely to internalize this feedback, resulting in negative symptom manifestation. The experience of rejection, discrimination, or having no sense of belonging with mainstream peers, may lead adolescents to find or accept social networks that in some way fulfill the need to belong, be accepted, and feel respected. In some instances, social networks confirm and reinforce negative and antisocial beliefs, which for some youth may provide a false sense of belonging and need fulfillment.

Gang Involvement

Numerous studies have revealed that gang membership is a high-risk lifestyle related to health risk behaviors (Pyrooz & Sweeten, 2015; Hennigan, Kolnick, Vindel, & Maxson, 2015; O'Brien, Daffern, Chu, & Thomas, 2013). Some of these adverse health risk behaviors include "juvenile delinquency, substance abuse, unsafe sex, gun carrying, illicit drug sales, arrest, nonfatal intentional injury, homicide, and educational, economic, and familial hardship" (Pyrooz & Sweeten, 2015, p. 414). The spread of gangs and violence perpetuated by gangs is a major challenge in economically disadvantaged communities across not only the United States, but the world in general (Hennigan et al., 2015). Estimates of youth gang involvement vary depending on the country, but approximately 10% to 19% of youth age 12 to 16 are likely to join gangs in high-risk areas of the United States (Hennigan et al., 2015).

Despite residing in communities riddled with gang activity, many youths who engage in delinquent or criminal behavior do not become involved with gangs (O'Brien et al., 2013). It appears that it takes more to convince a youth to become involved in a gang than to simply engage in violence (O'Brien et al., 2013). Extant literature suggests that youth involved in gangs exhibit more risky-attitudes and behaviors. The process of joining or participating in a gang is dynamic in that affiliation is sustained and motivated by the influence of group dynamics. How much a gang-involved youth identifies with the gang tends to mediate participation in crime and violence, regardless of whether the youth perceives he/she is likely to get caught and punished (O'Brien et al., 2013). Essentially, the youths cognitive and emotional ties to the gang, overshadow his/her intrapersonal tendencies.

Research suggests that gang involvement seems to be fairly fluid and transitory in that most youth remain a part of a gang for less than 4 years (O'Brien et al., 2013). In fact, most gang-involved youth in America and across the world remain active members for only 1 to 2 years (as cited in O'Brien et al., 2013). Youth membership peaks in mid-adolescence and wanes into early adulthood, which is consistent with the notion of fluidity and transition related to gang involvement.

The stereotypical gang-involved youth is a young male, from an ethnic or minority background, living in a large city or urban area (as cited in O'Brien et al., 2013). In one study, it was found that youth gang members were disproportionately male, black, Hispanic, from single-parent households, and of families living below the poverty level (Pyrooz & Sweeten, 2015). Data revealing that "approximately one-third of gang members are female, that gangs are arising from nonurban areas, and that the racial and ethnic composition of gangs mirrors the community" directly challenges the aforementioned stereotypical image of gang-involved youth (O'Brien et al., 2013, p.420).

According to O'Brien and colleagues (2013) the selection model suggests that gangs attract a specific type of individual. Essentially, gangs tend to attract individuals with a proclivity for delinquency and/or those who engage in crime regardless of affiliation. On the other hand, the facilitation model postulates that gangs are a specific type of group that promotes delinquency (O'Brien et al., 2013). In this instance gang membership would be the main cause of delinquent behavior, influenced by group processes and the normative structure of the group (O'Brien et al., 2013). Finally, the enhancement model suggests that a combination of selection and facilitation effects is what fuels the connection between gang affiliation and engagement in socially deviant behaviors. Basically, gangs select individuals who tend to exhibit deviant behavior, and at the same time the dynamics of the group enhances involvement in delinquent or criminal activity.

Keeping with the discussion of the impact of relationships on behavior, it is not surprising that involvement with negative peer social networks, having friends who are involved in gangs, and generally negative peer influences are reliable predictors of gang membership (O'Brien et al., 2013). Involvement with gangs or antisocial peers limits ones interactions with prosocial peers, this in turn limits chances for prosocial modeling and the development of positive social networks that would generally promote desistance from delinquent and criminal behavior (O'Brien et al., 2013; Pyrooz & Sweeten, 2015). The powerful impact of adolescent social networks on attitudes and behavior is quite evident, thus associating with delinquent peers may facilitate involvement with gangs or engagement in deviant behaviors by reinforcing and confirming negative or antisocial beliefs (O'Brien et al., 2013).

Case Scenario

Apply the knowledge that you have gained from this chapter to the case of Brianna (See *Case Scenario Brianna*). This is a case of an isolated and suicidal adolescent, who is seen for therapy by Amanda, a counselor. First read through Case Scenario *Brianna*, then use your counseling skills to answer the questions posed in Exercise *Amanda* with a partner (See *Exercise Amanda*). Afterwards, continue reading the subsequent sections for a thorough clinical review of the case.

Case Scenario - *Brianna*

Brianna is a 14-year-old Latino female who is coming to counseling at the request of her mother, Sara. Both Sara and Brianna speak English as their second language. Sara received a call from Brianna's school that Brianna had not been to school in over two weeks. She has also noticed that her daughter is spending more time in her room, not coming down for dinner, and is wearing long sleeves despite it still being summer. She is worried that Brianna might be cutting her wrists again.

Brianna was psychiatrically hospitalized two years prior for cutting her wrists and reporting suicidal thoughts. She spent 10 days in a psychiatric hospital. She reported no prior suicide attempts, however she admitted to her mother that she had been having infrequent suicidal thoughts since school began one month ago. She stated she felt suicidal because "nobody" liked her at school. Brianna was new at the school and was having trouble making friends, she felt isolated in the lunchroom and at recess time because she sat alone. Difficulty arose for her when she tried to make friends because of the language barrier between herself and her peers.

When Sara and Brianna got to the counseling center and met Amanda, their provider, Sara asked Amanda in Spanish if she speaks Spanish and Amanda replied "no." At that point, Sara and Brianna begin speaking English; however, they spoke very slowly and unclearly. Amanda had trouble understanding them and began feeling anxious because the session is took longer than her allotted hour time frame. Amanda decided not to use her standard structured assessment form that asked questions regarding suicidal thoughts, depression, and cutting because she did not believe Brianna and her mother would understand. Additionally, she wanted to save time. Thus, she used no structured form to guide her assessment and so doing she forgot to assess Brianna for her risk of suicide. Amanda, feeling as though the assessment went better than she thought it would, decided Brianna was simply depressed and in need of individual counseling on a weekly basis She scheduled Brianna for an appointment the following week and the assessment was complete in just over an hour. The next day Amanda received a call from the police who inform her that Brianna killed herself three hours after the counseling session.

Exercise 1 - *Amanda*

With a partner, answer the following questions pertaining to the actions of Amanda as the service provider:

1) Where was Amanda negligible in her services to Brianna and her mother?
2) At what point in counseling should Amanda have made the decision to refer?
3) Under what circumstances should Amanda had deviated from the use of the structured assessment form?
4) What are the legal and ethical issues in this case?

Clinical Review of Case

This is a case of negligible counseling services. Amanda, the responsible party in this case, should have made the decision to refer Brianna to a provider who was able to speak Spanish. To the degree possible, Amanda should have offered interpretive services at the moment she realized that there was such a language barrier. From the very moment Brianna and Sara entered therapy it was clear to all parties that such a language barrier existed (e.g., Amanda is asked if she speaks Spanish, Amanda does not understand them, Amanda chooses not to use her standard assessment form because the questions are in English). In addition, Amanda felt anxious about the services, yet she continued therapy. Additionally, Amanda gathered no information regarding Brianna's past psychiatric history (e.g., never asked about prior suicidal thoughts, attempts, cutting, or depression). She also failed to consult with previous providers about Brianna's care. The problem was that Amanda did not understand Brianna so she decided not to ask the needed and difficult questions that would have created a therapeutic atmosphere. As Amanda felt pressured to end the session promptly at one hour, she could have extended the session to gather the needed information to make an accurate assessment and diagnoses.

Conclusion

Culture is at the very center of human experience. This chapter highlighted the impact that culture has on adolescents during their time of development. It focused specifically on cultural factors that present themselves in the lives of adolescents, showing how culture can change the way adolescents experience life and other people. Within the topic of culture, it was important to focus the reader on different cultural contexts that are influential to an adolescent's development—family, school, neighborhood. Additionally, this chapter focused on the importance of considering how adolescents form a self-identity, as this is one of the hallmarks of adolescence. This chapter focused on how adolescents create self-autonomy and develop into early adulthood based on their racial and ethnic backgrounds. Collectivist and individualistic cultures have a lot to do with these differences, as one promotes the group and the other promotes the individual, respectively.

Overall the cultural, developmental, and environmental impact on delinquent and criminal behavior was discussed. While there are likely some intrapersonal traits and familial formats that are conducive to socially unacceptable behaviors, there are concomitant relational factors that contribute to adolescents behaving in socially unacceptable ways. Parenting, mental health, peer pressure, group status, economic status, and community environment are all factors that influence the development of positive and negative adolescent identities. Overwhelmingly, where the adolescent feels a sense of belonging and with whom provides that sense directs his/her behavior. Peer pressure, economic and community status, and group dynamics are great influencers of whether youth become involved in gangs and to what extent they identify with said gang.

The importance of friendships and social supports on an adolescent's development cannot be overstated. These relationships are greatly needed to help adolescents feel accepted and a place of belonging. In addition, they are crucial to helping them to create a self- identity. As such, identity forms, many times, based on external input (i.e., adolescents seek feedback on who they are as a person, which assigns meaning to their lives). When relationships are not present there are serious risk factors to adolescent development (e.g., depression, bullying, suicidal thoughts).

Chapter Keystones

- Providers should be aware of cultural differences and their affects on adolescent development in general. Culture likely impacts how adolescents develop and express moral reasoning and their self-identity.
- Adolescence represents the period in life between childhood and adulthood, and during this stage, adolescents are learning to navigate terrain of who they are, who they want to be, who they think they should be, and from where they have come.
- The pursuit of self-identity entails factors related to self-esteem, materialism, acculturation, and gender. Generally, one's cultural upbringing and his/her self-identity are inextricably bound.
- Justice involved youths' engagement in deviant behaviors is often due to developmental and environmental factors. Counselors should examine how cultural, socio-ecological, and interpersonal factors of an individual may lend to the development of delinquent and criminal behaviors in adolescence.
- Trauma, childhood maltreatment, and negligible parenting styles are also important factors to consider when working with justice involved youth. Not only can these factors contribute to a youths engagement in deviant behaviors, these factors have important implications on the youths ability to develop healthy social and self-identities.

- Providers should understand the social development of adolescents and how negative and positive factors in development can impact an individual's self-identity.
- Friendships and relating to others is an important aspect of being an adolescent. Individuals learn more about themselves and the world in how they relate to others. Counselors should understand the risk and protective factors related to friendship and group formation, and how this may influence the developing adolescent. Peer pressure and rejection are among the notable influences in adolescent interpersonal and social development.
- The process of gang involvement is influenced by both group processes and individual proclivities. Counselors should be aware that while the typical image of gang-involved youth exists, females can also be involved in gangs, there are a number of gangs emerging from nonurban communities, and the racial and ethnic makeup of the gang often reflects the community.

REFERENCES

Adams, R. E., & Cantin, S. (2013). Self-Disclosure in Friendships as the Moderator of the Association between Peer Victimization and Depressive Symptoms in Overweight Adolescents. *Journal of Early Adolescence, 33*(3), 341-362.

American Counseling Association (2014). ACA Code of Ethics. Alexandria, VA: Author.

American Psychiatric Association. (2013). *Diagnostic and statistical manual of mental disorders* (5th ed.). Arlington, VA: American Psychiatric Publishing.

Arnett, J. J. (2002). The psychology of globalization. American Psychologist, 57, 774–783.

Asakawa, K., & Csikszentmihalyi, M. (2000). Feelings of connectedness and internalization of values in Asian American adolescents. *Journal of Youth and Adolescence, 29*(2), 121-145. Retrieved from http://search.proquest.com/docview/204653034?accountid=34899.

Bae, Y. (1999). Human development: Theories and learning futures. *Futurics, 23*(3), 12-33. Retrieved from http://search.proquest.com/docview/219813343?accountid=34899.

Ballard, E. D. (2012). *Suicide risk in children and adolescents in a pediatric emergency department: Effects of race, income, gender, and age.* (Order No. 3544239, The Catholic University of America). *ProQuest Dissertations and Theses,* 89-n/a. Retrieved from http://search.proquest.com/docview/1221255194?accountid=34899. (1221255194).

Barrio, C. A. (2007). Assessing suicide risk in children: Guidelines for developmentally appropriate interviewing. *Journal of Mental Health Counseling, 29*(1), 50-66. Retrieved from http://search.proquest.com/docview/198670267?accountid=34899.

Barsano, C. A. (2005). *The stability of attachment patterns during adolescence.* (Order No. 3177403, The Chicago School of Professional Psychology). *ProQuest Dissertations and Theses,* 94-94 p. Retrieved from http://search.proquest.com/docview/305373793?accountid=34899. (305373793).

Bennett, D. L., Chown, P., & Kang, M. S. -. (2005). Cultural diversity in adolescent health care. *Medical Journal of Australia,183*(8), 436-8. Retrieved from http://search.proquest.com/docview/235727447?accountid=34899.

Berk, L. (2008). *Infants, children, and adolescents (6th edition).* Boston, MA: Pearson Education, Inc.

Berman, S. L., You, Y., Schwartz, S., Teo, G., & Mochizuki, K. (2011). Identity exploration, commitment, and distress: A cross national investigation in china, Taiwan, Japan, and the united states. *Child & Youth Care Forum, 40*(1), 65-75. doi: 10.1007/s10566-010-9127-1.

Besic, N., & Kerr, M. (2009). Punks, Goths, and Other Eye-Catching Peer Crowds: Do They Fulfill a Function for Shy Youths?. *Journal Of Research On Adolescence (Wiley-Blackwell), 19*(1), 113-121. doi:10.1111/j.1532-7795.2009.00584.x.

Biro, F. M., M.D., & Dorn, L. D., PhD. (2005). Puberty and adolescent sexuality. *Pediatric Annals, 34*(10), 777-84. Retrieved from http://search.proquest.com/docview/217550835?accountid=34899.

Bowers, K. (2014). You Know the Type. *Working Mother, 37*(4), 58-62.

Brand, M. (2004). Collectivistic versus individualistic cultures: a comparison of American, Australian and Chinese music education students' self-esteem. *Music Education Research, 6*(1), 57-65. doi:10.1080/1464380032000182830.

Brownell, C. (2013). Early development of prosocial behavior: Current perspectives. Infancy, 18, 1-9.doi: 10.1111/infa.12004.

Buddhism. (1999, 12). *Canada and the World Backgrounder.* 6-11. Retrieved from http://search.proquest.com/docview/210198923?accountid=34899.

Buddhism in North America. (2010). In Charles H. Lippy, & Peter W. Williams (Eds.), *Encyclopedia of Religion in America.* (pp. 314-322). Washington, DC: CQ Press. doi: http://0-dx.doi.org.library.regent.edu/10.4135/9781608712427.n55.

Buss, A. H. & Warren, W.L. (2000).Aggression Questionnaire: Manuel. Los Angeles CA: Western Psychological Services.

Butler, J. L. (1997). *Factors influencing diagnosis of ethnic minority inpatients in public facilities.* (Order No. 9727637, California School of Professional Psychology - Los Angeles). *ProQuest Dissertations and Theses,* 284-284. Retrieved from http://search.proquest.com/docview/304350011?accountid=34899. (304350011).

Campos, R. C., Besser, A., & Blatt, S. J. (2013). Recollections of Parental Rejection, Self-Criticism and Depression in Suicidality.*Archives Of Suicide Research*, *17*(1), 58-74. doi:10.1080/13811118.2013.748416.

Çam, Z., Seydoogullari, S., Çavdar, D., & Çok, F. (2012). Classical and contemporary approaches for moral development*.*Kuram Ve Uygulamada Egitim Bilimleri, 12*(2), 1222-1225. Retrieved from http://search.proquest.com/docview/1022332876?accountid=34899.

Canales, A. (2014). Models of Christian Leadership in Youth Ministry. *Religious Education*, *109*(1), 24. doi:10.1080/00344087.2014.868207.

Carlo, G., Eisenberg, N., & Knight, G. P. (1992). An objective measure of adolescents' prosocial moral reasoning. Journal of Research on Adolescence, 2, 331-349.

Carlo, G., Fabes, R., Laible, D., and Kupanoff, K. (1999). Early Adolescence and Prosocial/Moral Behavior II: The Role of Social and Contextual Influences. *Journal of Early Adolescence*, *19*(2), 133-147. doi:10.1177/0272431699019002001.

Chaplin, L. N., Hill, R. P., & John, D. R. (2014). Poverty and materialism: A look at impoverished versus affluent children. *Journal of Public Policy & Marketing, 33*(1), 78. Retrieved from http://search.proquest.com/docview/1532259699?accountid=34899.

Charmaraman, L., & Grossman, J. M. (2010). Importance of race and ethnicity: An exploration of Asian, black, Latino, and multiracial adolescent identity. *Cultural Diversity and Ethnic Minority Psychology, 16*(2), 144-151. doi:http://dx.doi.org/10.1037/a0018668.

Chen, C., & Farruggia, S. (2002). Culture and adolescent development. In W. J. Lonner, D. L. Dinnel, S. A. Hayes, & D. N. Sattler (Eds.), *Online Readings in Psychology and Culture* (Unit 11, Chapter 2), Center for Cross-Cultural Research, Western Washington University, Bellingham, Washington USA. Retrieved from http://www.wwu.edu/culture/Chen_Farruggia.htm.

Chen, H. (2012). Impact of parent's socioeconomic status on perceived parental pressure and test anxiety among Chinese high school students. *International Journal of Psychological Studies, 4*(2), 235-245. Retrieved from http://search.proquest.com/docview/1020571825?accountid=3489.

Chen, H., & Lan, W. (1998). Adolescents' perceptions of their parents' academic expectations: Comparison of American, Chinese-American, and Chinese high school students. *Adolescence, 33*(130), 385-90. Retrieved from http://search.proquest.com/docview/195943971?accountid=34899.

Cherry, K. (2014). *Erikson's Stages of Psychosocial Development: Psychosocial Development in Young Adulthood, Middle Age, and Old Age.* Retrieved from http://psychology.about.com/od/psychosocial theories/a/psychosocial_3.htm.

Chishti, P., Stone, D. H., Corcoran, P., Williamson, E., & Petridou, E. (2003). Suicide mortality in the European Union. *European Journal Of Public Health,13*(2), 108.

Choudhury, S. (2010). Culturing the adolescent brain: what can neuroscience learn from anthropology?. *Social Cognitive & Affective Neuroscience, 5*(2/3), 159-167.

Christie-Mizell, C. (2003). Bullying: The consequences of interparental discord and child's self-concept. *Family Process, 42*(2), 237-51. Retrieved from http://search.proquest.com/docview/218896678?accountid=34899.

Council for Accreditation of Counseling and Related Educational Programs (CACREP). (2009). 2009 standards for accreditation. Alexandria, VA: Author.

Crane, J., Winsler, A., & Sands, B. (2013). Patterns of referral recommendations for ethnically diverse children in subsidized child care. *Exceptional Children, 80*(1), 45-64. Retrieved from http://search.proquest.com/docview/1430460433?accountid=34899.

Crenshaw, W., & Markley, B. (2010). Double take: Peer pressure will persist through adolescence. *Daily Journal World,* Retrieved from http://search.proquest.com/docview/749808634?accountid=34899.

Cross, S. E., & Madson, L. (1997). Models of the self: Self-constructs and gender. *Psychological Bulletin, 122*(1), 5-37.

Downie, M., Mageau, G. A., & Koestner, R. (2008). What makes for a pleasant social interaction? motivational dynamics of interpersonal relations. *The Journal of Social Psychology, 148*(5), 523-34. Retrieved from http://search.proquest.com/docview/199805165?accountid=34899.

Ekerbicer, H. C., Celik, M. M., Kiran, H. H., & Kiran, G. G. (2007). Age at menarche in Turkish adolescents in Kahramanmaras, Eastern Mediterranean region of Turkey. *European Journal Of Contraception & Reproductive Health Care, 12*(3), 289-293.

Espelage, D. L., Bosworth, K., & Simon, T. R. (2000). Examining the social context of bullying behaviors in early adolescence. *Journal of Counseling and Development: JCD, 78*(3), 326-333. Retrieved from http://search.proquest.com/docview/219021014?accountid=34899.

Feinberg, R. (1988). Margaret Mead and Samoa: Coming of age in fact and fiction. *American Anthropologist*, New Series, *90*(3) pp. 656-663. Published by: Wiley on behalf of the American Anthropological Association, Article Stable URL: http://0-www.jstor.org.library.regent.edu/stable/678229.

Ferguson, E., Hagaman, J. A., Maurer, S. B., Mathews, P., & Peng, K. (2013). Asian culture in transition: is it related to reported parenting styles and transitivity of simple choices?. *Journal Of Applied Social Psychology, 43*(4), 730-740. doi:10.1111/jasp.12001.

Freeman, D. (1983). *Margaret Mead and Samoa: The making and unmaking of an anthropological myth*. Cambridge: Harvard University Press.

Friedlander, L. J., Connolly, J. A., Pepler, D. J., & Craig, W. M. (2007). Biological, familial, and peer influences on dating in early adolescence. *Archives of Sexual Behavior, 36*(6), 821-30. doi:http://dx.doi.org/10.1007/s10508-006-9130-7.

Garrett, A. D., & McCoy, H. (2007). Black adolescent racial identity and respectability. *Negro Educational Review, 58*(1), 35-48,131. Retrieved from http://search.proquest.com/docview/219038208?accountid=34899.

Golchin, N. A. H., Hamzehgardeshi, Z., Fakhri, M., & Hamzehgardeshi, L. (2012). The experience of puberty in Iranian adolescent girls: A qualitative content analysis. *BMC Public Health, 12*(698), 1-8. doi:10.1186/1471-2458-12-698.

Golberg, H., Paradis, J., & Crago, M. (2008). Lexical Acquisition over Time in Minority First Language Children Learning English as a Second Language. *Applied Psycholinguistics*, *29*(1), 41-65.

Goldberg, O. (2005). Adolescence: A time of change for children, parents. *Canadian Jewish News* Retrieved from http://search.proquest.com/docview/351417967?accountid=34899.63.1.14.

Hair, Jager, & Garret. (2002). *Helping Teens Develop Healthy Social Skills and Relationships: What the Research Shows about Navigating Adolescence.* Retrieved from http://www.hhs.gov/ash/oah/oah-initiatives/ta/paf_training2_healthysocialskills.pdf.

Heathfield, S. (2014). *Interpersonal Communication Dynamics.* retrieved from http://humanresources.about.com/od/interpersonalcommunicatio1/qt/com_com5.htm.

Higa, T. A. F., & Brandon, P. R. (2008). Participatory evaluation as seen in a Vygotskian framework. *The Canadian Journal of Program Evaluation, 23*(3), 103-125. Retrieved from http://search.proquest.com/docview/1038936431?accountid=34899.

Hennigan, K., Kolnick, K., Vindel, F., & Maxson, C. (2015). Targeting youth at risk for gang involvement: Validation of a gang risk assessment to support individualized secondary prevention. Children and Youth Services Review, 56, 86-96.

Hunt, L. M., & de Voogd, K.,B. (2007). Are good intentions good enough?: Informed consent without trained interpreters. *Journal of General Internal Medicine, 22*(5), 598-605. doi:http://dx.doi.org/10.1007/s11606-007-0136-1.

Ipenburg, A. (2012). Indonesia. In M. Juergensmeyer, & W. Roof (Eds.), *Encyclopedia of global religion.* (pp. 557-561). Thousand Oaks, CA: SAGE Publications, Inc. doi: http://dx.doi.org.ezproxy.apollolibrary.com/10.4135/9781412997898.n337.

Jones, R. B. (2014). Friendship characteristics, psychosocial development, and adolescent identity formation. *Personal Relationships*, *21*(1), 51-67.

Kanagy, R. (2013). Cultural Values of Japan. Retrieved from http://moon.com/2013/08/cultural-values-of-japan/.

Kanchier, C. (2007, Apr 14). Individualist versus collectivist: Why it matters. *The Vancouver Sun.* Retrieved from http://search.proquest.com/docview/242072194?accountid=34899.

Kim-Gervey, C. (2008). *Identity stability: A new construct for understanding healthy development in ethnic minority adolescents.*(Order No. 3295341, New York University). *ProQuest Dissertations and Theses,* 97-n/a. Retrieved from http://search.proquest.com/docview/304527490?accountid=34899. (304527490).

Klimstra, T. (2013). Adolescent Personality Development and Identity Formation. *Child Development Perspectives*, *7*(2), 80-84. doi:10.1111/cdep.12017.

Knack, J. M., Tsar, V., Vaillancourt, T., Hymel, S., & McDougall, P. (2012). What protects rejected adolescents from also being bullied by their peers? The moderating role of peer-valued characteristics. *Journal Of Research On Adolescence (Wiley-Blackwell)*, *22*(3), 467-479. doi:10.1111/j.1532-7795.2012.00792.x.

Kroger, J. (1990). Ego structuralization in late adolescence as seen through early memories and ego identity status. *Journal of Adolescence, 13*(1), 65-77.

Lapsley, D., & Carlo, G. (2014). Moral development at the crossroads: New trends and possible futures. *Developmental Psychology, 50*(1), 1-7. doi:10.1037/a0035225.

Lester, L., Waters, S., & Cross, D. (2013). The Relationship Between School Connectedness and Mental Health During the Transition to Secondary School: A Path Analysis. *Australian Journal Of Guidance & Counseling*, *23*(2), 157-171. doi:10.1017/jgc.2013.20.

Liu, R. B. (2014). Rejection Sensitivity and Depression: Mediation by Stress Generation. *Psychiatry: Interpersonal & Biological Processes*, *77*(1), 86-97.

Lloyd, B. T. (2002). A conceptual framework for examining adolescent identity, media influence, and social development. *Review of General Psychology, 6*(1), 73-91. doi:10.1037/1089-2680.6.1.73.

Lopez, S. (2011). Culture as an influencing factor in adolescent grief and bereavement. *Prevention Researcher*, *18*(3), 10-13.

Lorenzo-Blanco, E., Unger, J., Baezconde-Garbanati, L., Ritt-Olson, A., & Soto, D. (2012). Acculturation, Enculturation, and Symptoms of Depression in Hispanic Youth: The Roles of Gender, Hispanic Cultural Values, and Family Functioning. *Journal Of Youth & Adolescence*, *41*(10), 1350-1365.

Mackey, E., & La Greca, A. M. (2008). Does this make me look fat? Peer crowd and peer contributions to adolescent girls' weight control behaviors. *Journal Of Youth And Adolescence*, *37*(9), 1097-1110.

Massimini, F., & Delle Fave, A. (2000). Individual development in a bio-cultural perspective. *American Psychologist, 55*(1), 24-33. doi:10.1037/0003-066X.55.1.24.

Mayer, K., Makadon, H., & Garofalo, R. (2014). Promoting the successful development of sexual and gender minority youths. *American Journal Of Public Health*, *104*(6), 976-981.

McMahon, E. M., Reulbach, U., Keeley, H., Perry, I. J., & Arensman, E. (2010). Bullying victimization, self-harm and associated factors in Irish adolescent boys. *Social Science & Medicine*, *71*(1)1300-1307.

Mead, M. (1953). *Coming of age in Samoa; a psychological study of primitive youth for Western civilization. With a foreword by Franz Boas and a new pref. by the author*. (New York) Modern Library, 1953.

Mehta, T. G. (2005). *Multiple selves in south Asian adolescents.* (Order No. 3177361, University of Denver). *ProQuest Dissertations and Theses*, 145-145 p. Retrieved from http://search.proquest.com/docview/304993395?accountid=34899. (304993395).

Merriam-Webster. (2014). *Competent.* Retrieved from http://www.merriam-webster.com/dictionary/competent.

Merriam-Webster. (2014). *Morality*. Retrieved from http://www.merriam-webster.com/dictionary/morality.

Mulla, Z., & Krishnan, V. (2014). Karma-Yoga: The Indian Model of Moral Development. *Journal Of Business Ethics*, *123*(2), 339-351.

Murray, K. E., Klonoff, E. A., Garcini, L. M., Ullman, J. B., Wall, T. L., & Myers, M. G. (2014). Assessing acculturation over time: A four-year prospective study of Asian American young adults. *Asian American Journal Of Psychology*, *5*(3), 252-261.

National Association of the Deaf (NAD). (2008). *28 C.F.R. § 36.303(c): Effective Communication* Retrieved from http://www.nad.org/sites/default/files/admin/NAD%20Comments%20on%20ADA%20Title%20III%20DOJ%20NPRM%20081808.pdf.

Oberle, E., Schonert-Reichl, K., & Zumbo, B. D. (2011). Life satisfaction in early adolescence: Personal, neighborhood, school, family, and peer influences. *Journal of Youth and Adolescence, 40*(7), 889-901. Retrieved from http://search.proquest.com/docview/873526085?accountid=34899.

O'Brien, K., Daffern, M., Chu, C., &Thomas, S. (2013). Youth gang affiliation, violence, and criminal activities: A review of motivational, risk, and protective factors. Aggression and Violent Behavior, 18, 417-425.

O'Grady, K. (2006). The development of beliefs and values in early adolescence: a case study through religious education pedagogy. *International Journal Of Children's Spirituality*, *11*(3), 315-327.

Ozdemir F, Nazik E, Pasinlioglu, T. (2010). Determination of the motherly reactions to adolescents' experience of menarche. *J Pediatr Adolesc Gynecol. 23*(3), 153–157.

Peake, S. J., Dishion, T. J., Stormshak, E. A., Moore, W. E., & Pfeifer, J. H. (2013). Risk-taking and social exclusion in adolescence: Neural mechanisms underlying peer influences on decision-making. *NeuroImage, 82*(1), 23-34.

Pedersen, W. (2014). Forbidden Fruit? A Longitudinal Study of Christianity, Sex, and Marriage. *Journal Of Sex Research*, *51*(5), 542-550.

Platt, B., Kadosh, K. C., & Lau, J. Y. F. (2013). The role of peer rejection in adolescent depression. *Depression and Anxiety, 30*(9), 809-21.

Prinstein, M. J., & Julie, W. A. (2004). Cognitive moderators of the longitudinal association between peer rejection and adolescent depressive symptoms. *Journal of Abnormal Child Psychology, 32*(2), 147-58. Retrieved from http://search.proquest.com/docview/204989570?accountid =34899.

Pyrooz, D. & Sweeten, G. (2015). Gang membership between ages 5 and 17 years in the United States. Journal of Adolescent Health, 56, 414-419.

Quinlan, N. P. (2009). *A phenomenological case study of the multicultural counseling experience of students and faculty in relation to their perceptions of their multicultural competency and CACREP standards.* (Order No. 3356759, Old Dominion University). *ProQuest Dissertations and Theses,* 296-n/a. Retrieved from http://search.proquest.com/docview/ 305068250?accountid=34899. (305068250).

Rajiva, M. (2006). Brown girls, white worlds: Adolescence and the making of racialized selves*. *The Canadian Review of Sociology and Anthropology, 43*(2), 165-183. Retrieved from http://search.proquest.com/docview/ 234926096?accountid=34899.

Rhee, E., Uleman, J. S., Lee, H. K., & Roman, R. J. (1995). Spontaneous self-descriptions and ethnic identities in individualistic and collectivistic cultures. *Journal of Personality and Social Psychology, 69*(1), 142-152.

Rotheram-Borus, M. J. (1989). Ethnic differences in adolescents' identity status and associated behavior problems. Journal of Adolescence, *12*(1), 361–374.

Rudolph, J. J. (2014). Parent relationships and adolescents' depression and social anxiety: Indirect associations via emotional sensitivity to rejection threat. *Australian Journal Of Psychology*, *66*(2), 110-121.

Satomi, I. T., Ogawa, T., & Wilson, J. (2002). Moral development of Japanese kindergartners. *International Journal of Early Childhood, 34*(2), 12. Retrieved from http://search.proquest.com/docview/194793546?accounted =3489.

Schnitker, S. A., Felke, T. J., Barrett, J. L., & Emmons, R. A. (2014). Longitudinal study of religious and spiritual transformation in adolescents attending young life summer camp: Assessing the epistemic, intrapsychic, and moral sociability functions of conversion. *Psychology Of Religion And Spirituality*, *6*(2), 83-93.

Scholastic.com. (2014). *Why Social Skills are Key to Learning.* Retrieved from http://www.scholastic.com/parents/resources/article/social-emotional-skills/why-social-skills-are-key-to-learning.

Sentse, M., Dijkstra, J., Salmivalli, C., & Cillessen, A. N. (2013). The Dynamics of Friendships and Victimization in Adolescence: A Longitudinal Social Network Perspective. *Aggressive Behavior*, *39*(3), 229-238. Shankman, P. (2013). The "Fateful Hoaxing" of Margaret Mead A Cautionary Tale. *Current Anthropology*, *54*(1), 51-70.

Sijtsema. J. J., Lindenberg, S. M., & Veenstra, R. (2010). Do they get what they want or are they Stuck with what they can get? Testing homophily against default selection for friendships Of highly aggressive boys. The TRAILS study. Journal of Abnormal Child Psychology, *38*(1), 803-813.

Skapinakis, P., Bellos, S., Gkatsa, T., Magklara, K., Lewis, G., Araya, R., & Mavreas, V. (2011). The association between bullying and early stages of suicidal ideation in late adolescents in Greece. *BMC Psychiatry, 11*(1), 22.

Slattery, J. (2004). *Counseling diverse clients: Bringing context into therapy.* Belmont, CA: Thomson Brooks/Cole.

Soekarjo, D. D., de Pee, S. S., Bloem, M. W., Tjiong, R. R., Yip, R. R., Schreurs, W. P., & Muhilal. (2001). Socio-economic status and puberty are the main factors determining anemia in adolescent girls and boys in East Java Indonesia. *European Journal Of Clinical Nutrition*, *55*(11), 932.

Sohler, N. L., PhD., & Bromet, E. J., PhD. (2003). Does racial bias influence psychiatric diagnoses assigned at first hospitalization? *Social Psychiatry and Psychiatric Epidemiology, 38*(8), 463-72.

Steffens, M. C., & Jelenec, P. (2011). Separating implicit gender stereotypes regarding math and language: Implicit ability stereotypes are self-serving for boys and men, but not for girls and women. *Sex Roles, 64*(5-6), 324-335.

Stewart, S. M., Simmons, A., & Habibpour, E. (2012). Treatment of culturally diverse children and adolescents with depression. *Journal of Child and Adolescent Psychopharmacology, 22*(1), 72-9. doi:http://dx.doi.org/ 10.1089/cap.2011.0051. http://search.proquest.com/docview/305068250? accountid=34899. (305068250).

Stull, J. C. (2013). Family socioeconomic status, parent expectations, and a child's achievement. *Research in Education,* (90), 53-67. Retrieved from http://search.proquest.com/docview/1498088135?accountid=34899.

Swatos, W. (1998). *Adolescence/Youth Culture.* Retrieved from jhttp://hirr. hartsem.edu/ency/Adolescence.htm.

Terzini-Hollar, M. (2008). *Daily hassles, coping, and acculturation as predictors of psychological well-being among Korean-American adolescents.* (Order No. 3303100, Fordham University). *ProQuest Dissertations and Theses,* 185-n/a. Retrieved from http://search.proquest. com/docview/304639951?accountid=34899. (304639951.

The American Mental Health Counseling Association (AMHCA). (2010). *Principles for AMHCA Code of Ethics.* Retrieved from https://www. amhca.org/assets/news/AMHCA_Code_of_Ethics_2010_w_pagination_c xd_51110.pdf.

The Jason Foundation. (2014). *Youth Suicide Statistics.* Retrieved from http://jasonfoundation.com/prp/facts/youth-suicide-statistics/.

Theokas, C., Almerigi, J. B., Lerner, R. M., Dowling, E. M., Benson, P. L., Scales, P. C., et al. (2005). Conceptualizing and modeling developmental and ecological asset components of thriving in early adolescence. *Journal of Early Adolescence, 25*(1), 113-143.

Thomas, N. R., & Joseph, M. V. (2013). Positive adolescent development: Relevance of family interventions. *Rajagiri Journal of Social Development, 5*(2), 115-134. Retrieved from http://search.proquest.com/ docview/1547936006?accountid=34899.

Turner, I., Reynolds, K. J., Lee, E., Subasic, E., & Bromhead, D. (2014). Well-being, school climate, and the social identity process: A latent growth model study of bullying perpetration and peer victimization. *School Psychology Quarterly*, *29*(3), 320-335.

United Nations (UN). (2014). Definition of Youth. *un.org*. Retrieved from http://www.un.org/esa/socdev/documents/youth/fact-sheets/youth-definition.pdf.

U.S. Bureau of the Census (2010). “2010 Census.” Retrieved from http://www.census.gov/2010census/.

Vellymalay, S. K. N. (2012). Parental involvement at home: Analyzing the influence of parents' socioeconomic status. *Studies in Sociology of Science, 3*(1), 1-6. Retrieved from http://search.proquest.com/docview/1014276031?accountid=34899.

Vellymalay, S. K. N. (2013). Relationship between Malaya parents' socioeconomic status and their involvement in their children's education at home. *E-BANGI, 8*(1), 1-11. Retrieved from http://search.proquest.com/docview/1443352630?accountid=34899.

Vo-Jutabha, E. (2005). *The impact of historical, social, and cultural contexts on Vietnamese adolescent identity exploration.*(Order No. 3189859, Clark University). *ProQuest Dissertations and Theses,* 96-96 p. Retrieved from http://search.proquest.com/docview/305005520?accountid=34899. (305005520).

Wang, Y. (2012). Individualistic and collectivistic perspectives on patterns of teaching and learning: Products of culture. *Psychology Research, 1*(7), 53-58. Retrieved from http://search.proquest.com/docview/1443619315?accountid=34899.

World Health Organization (WHO). (2008). Social Cohesion for Mental Well-Being among Adolescents. Copenhagen: WHO Regional Office for Europe.

World Health Organization (WHO). (2014). Adolescent Development. *Who.int*. retrieved from http://www.who.int/maternal_child_adolescent/topics/adolescence/development/en/.

Yavuzer, Y., Karatas, Z., Civilidag, A., & Gundogdu, R. (2014). The Role of Peer Pressure, Automatic Thoughts and Self-Esteem on Adolescents' Aggression. *Eurasian Journal Of Educational Research (EJER)*, (54), 61-78.

Yoo, J. (2009). Peer influence on adolescent boys' appearance management behaviors. *Adolescence*, *44*(176), 1017-1031.

Young, R., Sproeber, N., Groschwitz, R. C., Preiss, M., & Plener, P. L. (2014). Why alternative teenagers self-harm: exploring the link between non-suicidal self-injury, attempted suicide and adolescent identity. *BMC Psychiatry*, *14*(1), 1-25.

Yukl, G. (2012). Effective Leadership Behavior: What We Know and What Questions Need More Attention. *Academy Of Management Perspectives*, *26*(4), 66-85.

Zajko, S. (2007). Adolescent Development and Psychology. *Peoplelearn.homestead.com*. Retrieved from http://peoplelearn.homestead.com/Adolescent_Development_and_Psychology.pdf.

Zhang, Y. (2013). The embodiment of individualistic values in American nationality. *Studies in Sociology of Science, 4*(3), 36-42. Retrieved from http://search.proquest.com/docview/1463675302?accountid=34899.

Zheng, T. (1999). *Margaret Mead.* Retrieved from http://classes.yale.edu/02-03/anth500a/projects/project_sites/99_zheng/kelly1.html.

Zhuang, G. (2013). A Survey of Modern Buddhist Culture in Shanghai. *Chinese Studies In History*, *46*(3), 79-94.

In: Juvenile Delinquency
Editor: Bonnie A. Nelson

ISBN: 978-1-63485-742-0
© 2016 Nova Science Publishers, Inc.

Chapter 2

DEVELOPMENTAL CONSIDERATIONS IN JUSTICE INVOLVED ADOLESCENTS

Lee A. Underwood*, PsyD, Frances L. L. Dailey, PhD, and Lisa O. Barras, MA

[1]Regent University School of Psychology and Counseling, VA, US
[2]Walden University, MN, US
[3]Southwestern University, TX, US

ABSTRACT

The dynamics characterizing adolescent development are unique and complex. Areas especially important in adolescence include academic functioning, moral reasoning and cognitive development. Issues in interpersonal decision-making include peer affiliation, fear of rejection, peer pressure, defensiveness and pessimism, and impression management. Additionally, friendships and group identity formation are crucial elements in adolescent interpersonal functioning. Adolescence is a time of individuation from family, evaluation of one's beliefs and experiences and experimentation of various roles and identities in the search for an integrated whole. In fact, the high school and college years have been described as a developmental moratorium wherein adolescents are given temporary freedom from responsibilities by society. Finally, it is crucial for juvenile justice providers to assess the implications of these multifaceted dynamics in their own clinical work in light of ethical and multicultural guidelines to work competently with the groups whom they

* E-mail: leeunde@regent.edu.

serve. The purpose of this chapter is to understand the major developmental theorist's view of critical developmental milestones, understand the social, biological and interpersonal effects on an adolescents' functioning; learn how rage, anger and delinquency are central components in the developing adolescents and skills to manage behavioral outbursts; identify aspects of depression and anxiety in adolescents and how these symptoms manifest into pathology; learn skills and tools to work with adolescents who struggle with these changes and adolescents who are defiant to the therapy process; identify markers related to low and inflated self-esteem and how it may disrupt adolescent development; improve awareness of friendship development and group identity contribute and its impact on decision making; and identify ethical and other best practice implications.

INTRODUCTION

The dynamics characterizing adolescent development are unique and complex. These aspects have direct implications for juvenile justice providers among those who work with justice involved adolescents. Some of the forces underlying important factors during adolescent development are emotional changes, biological changes and social/interpersonal changes. Considerations from developmental theorists are imperative to understanding adolescent development. Areas especially important in adolescence include academic functioning, moral reasoning and cognitive development. Issues in interpersonal decision-making include peer affiliation, fear of rejection, peer pressure, defensiveness and pessimism, and impression management. Additionally, friendships and group identity formation are crucial elements in adolescent interpersonal functioning. Particularly, the application of spiritual and moral values and beliefs in interpersonal decision making is an area worth exploring for those working with religiously inclined adolescents and families. Finally, it is crucial for juvenile justice providers to assess the implications of these multifaceted dynamics in their own treatment work in light of ethical and multicultural guidelines to work competently with the groups whom they serve.

Sigelman and Rider (2012) provide a review of identity development and its implications in the adolescent years. Adolescence has been identified as a period of identity formation and role transition (Sigelman & Rider, 2012). Whereas in childhood, self-concepts tend to be physical, concrete, and undifferentiated, adolescence is characterized by emerging self-concepts that are more psychological, abstract, multifaceted and integrated by comparison (Sigelman & Rider, 2012). In conjunction with a broadening of one's self-concept, adolescence becomes a time of increased self-awareness. This increased self-awareness forms the basis of both positive self-reflection as well as maladaptive levels of self-consciousness and self-deprecation (Sigelman & Rider, 2012). Struggles with self-esteem and social comparison become increasingly salient in adolescence, as adolescents deal with different sources of social stress in their lives (Sigelman & Rider, 2012).

Adolescents are constantly forging their sense of personal identity in various domains, including moral, ethnic, vocational, familial, and social identity. Adolescence is a time of individuation from family, evaluation of one's beliefs and experiences and experimentation of various roles and identities in the search for an integrated whole. In fact, the high school and college years have been described as a developmental moratorium wherein adolescents are given temporary freedom from responsibilities by society. Thus, adolescents have the ability to experiment with different roles and discover the men and women they desire to become (Sigelman & Rider, 2012). Factors such as personality, opportunities to explore, relationship with parents, cultural context, and cognitive development all become important in this process (Sigelman & Rider, 2012). It is in this context that adolescents experience the tumultuous noise of interpersonal relationships.

After reading this chapter, the reader will be able to:

- Understand the major developmental theorist's view of critical developmental milestones.
- Understand the social, biological and interpersonal effects on an adolescents' functioning.
- Learn how rage, anger and delinquency are central components in the developing adolescent and skills to manage behavioral outbursts.
- Identify aspects of depression and anxiety in adolescents and how these symptoms manifest into pathology.
- Learn skills and tools to work with adolescents who struggle with these changes and adolescents who are defiant to the therapy process.
- Identify markers related to low and inflated self-esteem and how it may disrupt adolescent development.
- Improve awareness of friendship development and group identity contribute and its impact on decision making.
- Identify ethical and other best practice implications.
- Apply knowledge gained from this chapter to case scenarios.

CONSIDERATIONS FROM PIAGET, ERIKSON AND MAHLER

In understanding cognitive and social development of an adolescent, it is highly important to understand the theories and ideas of previous researchers. Some of the most influential researchers to date are Piaget, Erikson and Mahler.

Table 2.1. Piaget's Theory of Cognitive Development

Age	Stage Described
Birth – 2 Years Old	Sensorimotor – Life is experienced through sensing and actions.
2 Years Old – 6 Years Old	Pre-operational – The individual is able to use words and images to describe needs.
7 Years Old – 11 Years Old	Concrete Operational – Concrete thinking, logical thinking, and ability to think about analogies.
12 Years Old and Beyond	Formal Operational – The ability to develop hypothetical scenarios and begin logical abstract thought.

Piaget's Cognitive Developmental Stages

Jean Piaget developed a theory of human cognitive development, defining several cognitive milestones that an individual should achieve as a part of normal human development. Piaget's stages describe how a normally developed person experiences the world and how their cognitive thinking begins to develop as they begin to age.

Piaget described his first stage being from birth to two years old where the child experiences life through sensing and feeling things, titled the sensorimotor stage (Ivy & Goncalves, 1988). Clearly this is the first stage of human life where an individual is building experiences and conclusions about the world. Next, from two years to six years, the child begins the preoperational stage in which the individual is able to describe their world using words and images (Ivy & Goncalves, 1988). In this stage the individual is able to vocalize needs and describe experiences. The next stage, from seven to 11 years old, the individual begins the concrete operational stage of cognitive development (Ivy & Goncalves, 1988). In this stage the child is now able to think concretely about their experiences and grasp analogies. Lastly, Piaget described his final stage as occurring during adolescence and continuing throughout life.

During adolescence the young person is now able to think more abstractly at improved rates of higher cognitive thought. It is at this stage of development that Piaget details his final and most complex cognitive thought process. Piaget described his final stage titled *formal operations* which is the stage that begins in adolescence and continues through life (Inhelder & Piaget, 1958). This stage is largely marked by the increased ability to develop logical thoughts and implement abstract ideas (Inhelder & Piaget, 1958). This is likely the first time in the adolescents' life when they are able to think this abstractly about ideas and themselves. The adolescent is able to think abstractly about their own personal experiences and develop thoughts that exist only in the mind, which is developed from maturation and experience (Inhelder & Piaget, 1958). As adolescents combine their experiences with new abstract thinking activities they are setting the stage for their continued development as this is the final stage of development in Piaget's theory, and it continues throughout the individuals' life.

Table 2.2. Erik Erikson's Theory of Adolescent Cognitive Development

Age Range	Stage	Description
12-20 Years Old	Identity vs Role Confusion	Coherent sense of self is developed. Feelings of confusion and indecisiveness.

Erikson's Psychosocial Development Stages

Erik Erikson developed a theory describing psychosocial stages of human life. Erikson described life stages in which an individual grows by relating, connecting, or disconnecting to others. The initial stage described by Erikson is titled, trust versus mistrust, from the age of birth to approximately 18 months (Hoare, 1991). In this life stage the individual must develop a loving relationship with their mother or caregiver to establish who trust is worthy and who is not. Next, from approximately 18 months old to three years old, the child begins to put energy into physical development such as walking or climbing, which is titled autonomy versus shame/doubt (Hoare, 1991). The next stage of development Erikson describes is called initiative versus guilt, and occurs from approximately three years of age to six years of age (Hoare, 1991). In this stage independence is imperative and the child begins to understand complex emotions, such as guilt. The last stage before adolescence is called industry versus inferiority (Hoare, 1991). This stage occurs from approximately six years to 12 years old and the overarching importance of this stage is to develop assertive skills and take initiative in their lives.

The psychosocial challenge occurring during adolescence developed by Erikson (1968) is titled *identity versus role confusion.* In this developmental stage the adolescent is in search for a sense of identity, which often develops in a crisis format (Erikson, 1968). The adolescent continues to develop the regularity of their everyday life, however striving to find individuality within ones' conscience (Erikson, 1968). The goal of this stage is to combine both what the adolescent identified with as a child along with reputing a new identity, which is titled identity achievement (Erikson, 1968). Once identity achievement is accomplished, the adolescent can develop their own sense of self in combination with the values instilled in them by their childhood caregivers.

Erikson described many situations in which the adolescent attempts to achieve a sense of identity in a variety of ways. Erikson recognized that many adolescents will take on other identities (*identity adoption*) as their own in order to achieve identity achievement. Often, adolescents impulsively adopt others' values, as their own. This is done without much consideration from the adolescent, without the adolescent sifting through their caregivers' ideals for what the adolescent deems as important to them individually (Erikson, 1968). When an adolescent adopts ideals or identities prior to analyzing through one's own desires, beliefs, and standards, they have achieved a stage called *foreclosure* (Erikson, 1968). Another identity adoption stage is *negative identity* which occurs when an adolescent adopts an identity that is opposite of what their families' expected of them (Erikson, 1968). For example, an adolescent who has a family that is expecting the adolescent to attend college for a degree in science, the adolescent may then decide to change his or her major to art degree. *Oppositional identity* describes a stage in which the adolescent exacerbates characteristics of oneself that might be perceived as a negative stereotype in order to refuse the dominant culture (Erikson, 1968). The adolescent in this stage might identify themselves with a group of people that skip school and use substances to reject dominant cultural ideals of attending school and getting good grades. At this time many adolescents may find themselves less committed to any values and become apathetic about their identity, thus experiencing *identity diffusion* (Erikson, 1968). Adolescents in this stage, often struggle with managing every day needs of life and find themselves without a job or avoiding schoolwork, due to a lack of focus on him or her and a lack of established values. Lastly, many adolescents might try several different identities in order to find their true selves as they enter *identity moratorium* (Erikson, 1968). Identity moratorium is a stage the adolescent recognizes the self they have adopted is temporary and may continue to adopt temporary identities until they find one that fits their individuality (Erikson, 1968).

MAHLER'S SEPARATION-INDIVIDUATION DEVELOPMENT

Self-awareness is imperative for adolescent development. Margaret Mahler (1975) described the belief that from birth to four months the child is unaware that they are an independent human being separate from their mothers [parent's] (Mahler, Pine, Fred, & Bergman). The first stage is titled the *autistic stage* where the child views him or herself as one with their mother, not as separate beings. Then after approximately four months, the child begins to develop a personality and sense of an individual self, independent from mother (Mahler, 1975). In this stage called the *symbiotic stage*, the child is able to begin to attach and form an emotional relationship (Hamachek, 1985). Next, the child begins *differentiation* from approximately six to nine months where the individual begins to understand physical boundaries (Hamachek, 1985). Then begins the stage titled, *practicing*, from approximately 10 to 16 months of age, where the child begins to develop autonomy from his or her mother (Hamachek, 1985). Next, at 17 to approximately 36 months of age, the individual begins to develop independence and also wants to regress to seeking his or her mother (Hamachek, 1985). This stage is titled, *reapproachment*, and can be difficult as the child wants the emotional connection, but only at times the child desires it (Hamachek, 1985). The final stage, *constancy*, begins at approximately 36 months and continues throughout life (Hamachek, 1985). During this stage the individual consolidates his or her identity and it becomes established separate from the mother. What we have learned from Mahler is that adolescent identity development includes past and present family dynamics, establishing a "self", and differentiating from one's family - a key component to normal development.

When considering the various areas of development and various models and stages, other areas of development must also be integrated into the adolescent's developmental experiences. These experiences comprise the remainder of this chapter.

EMOTIONAL DEVELOPMENT

During puberty, adolescents often experience rapid changes of emotions. Often researchers question why adolescents experience such a dramatic change in mood, especially depression, during their adolescent years (Berger, 2005).

Hormones are key chemical culprits in adolescent emotional changes that can evidence themselves in strong mood shifts, such as sadness, irritation, apathy and agitation. As such, it is imperative to understand the hormonal changes within the adolescents' body that impact the individual's mood. Often the biological changes often provide some anxiety for the adolescent, and as a result they might experience peer or adult reactions due to the biological changes, which often leads to an increase of emotions (Berger, 2005). When adolescent male's experience a deepening of his voice, is teased about this change by a sibling (for example), feelings of embarrassment, resentment, anger, or even sadness may be experienced. Of special concern to providers working with adolescents, is when negative emotions are direct inward - towards oneself, or outwards - towards others (Berger, 2005). An adolescent who internalizes emotions might harm him or herself, or abuse substances, whereas a young person who externalizes might destroy objects or injure others. The following section discusses problematic emotional reactions adolescents may experience and that are of therapeutic concern.

Disproportionate Rage, Anger and Delinquency Management

Often, during this time of elevated emotions, when many adolescents experience a spike in emotions, often leading to elevated anger and rage (Berger, 2005). The adolescent who is internalizing emotions might harm himself or herself by cutting their arms during moments of seemingly unmanageable anger. Those individuals that experience externalizing emotions might find him or herself vandalizing someone's property, or might act out violently against a person. A young person might act out in suicidal behavior at this time in order to "punish" someone that hurt them, which would also be externalizing their emotions and not internalizing emotions as it is often viewed (Berger, 2005). During expression of anger, it is typical for adolescents to rebel against parental authority. Many behavioral health providers find this to be natural occurrence, which is often expected (Berger, 2005). The concern for any rebellion might be when a young person might rebel in manners that are not law-abiding, thus leading to further and potentially life-long damages.

Considering the high levels of anger and rage experienced during adolescence and the possible negative implications that can occur as a result of the anger, it is imperative as a provider to find strategies to help these young people manage their anger. Hains (1992) completed research to identify the effects of coping strategies to deal with anger among adolescents. Research showed that those adolescents who were specifically trained in cognitive skills and relaxation skills to deal with anger and stress appeared to have reduced levels of anger and depression over one month after their training (Hains, 1992). It appears that providing the adolescents with specific coping skills to deal with their negative emotions greatly impacted the occurrence of negative emotions in the future. One of the coping skills used in the intervention was cognitive self-defeating thought stopping. Each adolescent were asked to think of an emotional event, think of their thoughts tied to that event, and identify the thoughts that were potentially self-defeating (Hains, 1992). In addition to learning cognitive skills, the adolescents learned progressive relaxation strategies and visual relaxation strategies (Hains, 1992). The adolescents learned how to avoid making their bodies tense during times of stress and anxiety, and how to visualize calming events when they might be upset (Hains, 1992). A major finding with this study shows that adolescents are better able to handle their times of anger and rage if they are taught preventative coping skills.

As a provider, it is important to have a base knowledge of the skills needed to work with adolescents that are experiencing angry emotions, as many of them might be defiant or resistant to the therapeutic process. Hanna, Hanna and Keys (1999) described a large variety of strategies that would assist a provider in working with angry or defiant adolescents. The authors described the importance of setting the example for the adolescent as in many cases the adolescent has not been able to observe many models for appropriate social behavior (Hanna, Hanna &Keys, 1999). A few of the overlying strategies in working with these adolescents are showing respect for the individual, being genuine, avoiding appearing as an expert, and providing humor when appropriate (Hanna, Hanna & Keys, 1999). The provider must develop the skills in relating to the adolescent while respecting their opinions and beliefs. The adolescent is likely to become increasingly more defiant if he or she believes that the provider is being judgmental of their ideas. The provider must also recognize how they are perceived by the adolescent, as often many adult figures present as an authority which can deeper the disconnect from the adolescent and the provider. In avoiding being the expert, the provider can provide appropriately timed humor to diffuse some of the adolescents' anger-oriented boundaries and develop a safe environment for the adolescent to open up to the provider.

Depression and Anxiety

Rates of depression and anxiety highly increase at the age of puberty. The U.S. Department of Health and Human Services (1999) published information describing the rates of depression and anxiety within the adolescent population. The results showed that 10% of the adolescents reported experiencing a form of anxiety within their life and 12% of the adolescents reported experiencing depression within their lives (U.S. Department of Health and Human Services [DHHS], 1999). In addition to these findings, it was found that 20% of the adolescents have experienced either a mental, behavioral, or emotional problem in their lives (DHHS, 1999). Dixon, Scheidegger, and McWhirter (2009) completed a study to identify the factors between the desire to matter to others in adolescents and the link between anxiety and depressions. Mattering to others was defined as feeling appreciated by others, having regular contact with friends and family, and gaining recognition from others. In addition, the research showed that during adolescent years an increase in anxiety was apparent, which was largely linked to an increase in depression (Dixon et al., 2009). When examining adolescent depression and anxiety, it is not as important to know "what comes first," however it does appear that anxiety is largely prevalent prior to symptoms of depression with adolescents.

Major hormonal changes occur within the adolescents' body during puberty, however other factors tend to increase the young person's depression, albeit a combination of relationship stress, family, identity crises, or academic pressures (Berger, 2005). However standard the emotional changes are, in many cases an adolescents' changes of mood might develop beyond the routine mood shifts and their angry emotions might lead to irresponsible behavior, or their sad emotions may lead to major depression resulting in suicide (Berger, 2005). Often adolescents experience distress in their lives in which they cannot view a brighter future, thus resulting in either suicidal ideation, parasuicide, or committed suicide (Berger, 2005). As a provider, it is imperative to assess any adolescent that describes suicidal ideations by the following factors to address whether the young person's thoughts may lead to suicidal behaviors: access to weapons, use of any substances, and lack of supervision (Berger, 2005).

In addition to the hormonal and interpersonal factors that may lead to adolescent depression, often genetic vulnerability or parental distress can lead to depression. A young person who has a parent that has experienced depression him or herself or experienced any psychiatric disorders has a higher likeliness of developing depression during adolescence (Berger, 2005). It is clear that there is a combination of a variety of factors that lead to depression in adolescence including interpersonal stress, identity crises, genetic factors, and relational factors (Berger, 2005).

Low or Inflated Self-Esteem

Research has shown that children and adolescents often gradually report feeling less self-assured every year (Jacobs et al., 2002). In an examination of 7th through 12th graders, self-esteem differed as a function of peer group affiliation. Individuals who were affiliated with a group of higher peer-rated status generally showed higher self-esteem than those associated with a peer group of lower status. Among those who did not affiliate with a peer group, but considered peer group affiliation important, self-esteem suffered and was low. There was also a subset of adolescents who did not consider peer group affiliation important (Brown & Lohr, 1987). Nonetheless, for those during childhood who did not report participation in a crowd or specific peer group (i.e., those that were not popular) the literature suggests that the majority of them reported having at least one close friend (Sigelman & Rider, 2012).

Group membership in specific crowds was predictive of adolescent risk behaviors such as cigarette use, alcohol use, and sexual intercourse in an examination of 8th graders in a multi-ethnic school. Specifically, the individuals who focused on grades and affiliated themselves with others who were like minded were least likely to participate in alcohol use and sexual intercourse, while other groups that did not focus on education as much were most likely to participate in these behaviors (Dolcini & Adler, 1994). Moreover, group membership was related to these behaviors above and beyond the effects of self-esteem (Dolcini & Adler, 1994) and availability of alcohol and drugs appeared to mediate whether students from specific crowds participated in cigarette and alcohol use (Dolcini & Adler, 1994). Finally, in an examination of seventh grade students using ecological momentary assessment of peer affiliations, perceptions of peer affiliates, mood, activities, and behaviors, Rusby, Westling, Crowley, and Light (2013) found that mood states were related to peer affiliations and perceptions. Specifically, happy moods tended to be associated with spending time with popular and desired peers. Sadness and anxiety were related to feeling left out of peer groups (Rusby et al., 2013). Finally, mood liability in relation to levels of perceived social acceptance was more drastic for girls than for boys, and this may relate to a higher importance placed by girls on social acceptance (Rusby et al., 2013).

Friendships and Group Identity Formation

The process of choosing friends in adolescence is complex and multifaceted, but it is possible to explore general principles regarding this process. Sigelman and Rider (2012) comment on the changing nature of social networks during adolescence. Within Western cultures, elementary-school children may begin showing interest in the opposite sex, having crushes, and talking about whom likes whom, it is not until adolescence that close opposite-sex relationships begin to form (Sigelman & Rider, 2012).

During childhood, social relationships are primarily same-sex relationships (Sigelman & Rider, 2012). However, the authors cite previous research identifying several transitions that occur during the adolescent years. First, boys and girls become members of same-sex groups or cliques that are isolated from same-sex groups of the opposite sex (Sigelman & Rider, 2012). Then, with same-sex cliques as a stable base, same-sex male and female groups begin to cross-over and begin interacting with one-another in early adolescence. By high school, a heterosexual crowd has formed and males and females are regularly interacting as friends (Sigelman & Rider, 2012). Finally, the crowd disappears in late high school once couples have formed and male-female (opposite sex) friendships are a regular occurrence (Sigelman & Rider, 2012).

It appears, then, that a major motivator of friendship choice during the adolescent years, conscious or otherwise, is preparation for dating and later intimate relationships, as well as building a stable support base from which that occurs. Sigelman and Rider (2012) outline previous research suggesting that dating during adolescence occurs in four phases. First, there is an initiation phase during early adolescence that is a self-focused period of proving that one is able to relate romantically with the opposite gender (Sigelman & Rider, 2012). Then, there is peer-focused status phase in which one gains status with peers by having a desirable romantic relationship (Sigelman & Rider, 2012). In late-adolescence, the individual's attention shifts to the relationship itself rather than peers or self-image during the affection phase (Sigelman & Rider, 2012). Finally, the move to early adulthood marks the bonding phase in which commitment becomes the focus (Sigelman & Rider, 2012). These concerns and dynamics increasingly become the focus of adolescents' interpersonal lives, and are thus important to understand.

In addition to dating and group formation dynamics, friendship choices are changing overall. Earlier, it was noted that adolescents' self-concepts change from a superficial to a psychological and abstract level during the transition to adolescence. Similarly friendship choices that were once based on common activities, superficial similarities and mutual caring and loyalty become increasingly based on higher virtues such as intimacy, disclosure, and other psychological characteristics (Sigelman & Rider, 2012). These may include interests, attitudes, values and general personality traits, for example (Sigelman & Rider, 2012). Finally, Sigelman & Rider (2012) note that intimacy in same-sex friendships remains high throughout adolescence, but intimacy in cross-sex friendships begins achieving a high level around eleventh grade (Sigelman & Rider, 2012).

Perhaps one of the most important factors to consider in examining friendship choice and group identity among adolescents is emerging patterns of homophiles, which is the tendency for individuals to spend time with others who are similar to them in some way. This has been discussed earlier in regards to various superficial and psychological characteristics. In one recent analysis, Currarini, Jackson, and Pin (2010) explored homphily among a sample of American high school students. Homophily is described by the authors as a normal component of many social networks. The authors examined homophily vis-à-vis race among high school students using a national survey, and they explored two sources: biases in preferences and biases in meeting rates of those considered members of the out group. Overall, the authors found strong evidence for the existence of such biases, with some groups (e.g., Asians and African Americans) biased toward interacting with members of their own race at rates much higher than other groups (e.g., Hispanics and Caucasians; Currarini, Jackson, & Pin, 2010). The authors found wide variability among various ethnic groups in the extent to which groups valued relationships with other groups. Specifically, Asians exhibited the least preference bias, with African Americans exhibited the most preference bias (Currarini, Jackson, & Pin, 2010). Clearly, patterns of homophily are complex and important to consider in dynamics of friendship choice.

Peer Affiliation

Adolescence is a time when the decisions that underlie peer affiliation become complex and multifaceted. Sigelman and Rider (2012) note the overall importance of being part of a peer group during the high school years. Despite the fact that peers generally have a negative influence on adolescent development, it seems that peer affiliation may have a more positive effect on behavior (Sigelman & Rider, 2012). The authors note that the extent to which peer affiliation leads to these positive outcomes depends on factors such as the type of crowd being affiliated with, the sense of dependence an adolescent has on their peers' acceptance of them, and the strength of the adolescent's relationship with their parents (Sigelman & Rider, 2012).

During childhood and adolescence, healthy friendship and peer affiliation is a crucial predictor of positive adult adjustment as well as happiness and social competence during the childhood and adolescent years (Sigelman & Rider, 2012). Moreover, it is important that friendships are with peers that are well adjusted, psychologically healthy, delinquent free and supportive (Sigelman & Rider, 2012). Finally, it appears that childhood friendships prepare individuals for later cross-gender friendships and dating during adolescence and early adulthood (Sigelman & Rider, 2012).

Fear of Rejection

The fear of rejection and the quest for popularity appear to be strongly influential processes in the lives of children and adolescents. As children and adolescents begin interacting with peers, factors such as physical attractiveness and cognitive ability have some influence into one's level of popularity. However, factors such as socially competent behavior and emotional regulation abilities may be more important (Sigelman & Rider, 2012). The outcomes of childhood popularity ratings become very important later in life. Adolescents are classified as popular (liked by most), rejected (disliked by most), neglected (neither liked nor disliked), controversial (liked by many and disliked by many), and average. For those classified as rejected in childhood, outcomes may include poor later adjustment, self-esteem and social skill deficits, lowered academic performance, negative perceptions of others and negative peer affiliate relations (Sigelman & Rider, 2012). For those classified as neglected, most attain greater acceptance later, although some suffer from social anxiety, victimization and other negative outcomes (Sigelman & Rider, 2012).

Rejection and dislike, as well as perceived rejection and dislike, have several different associations. In a meta-analytic review of over 23,000 children and adolescents, Card (2010) examined the outcomes of antipathetic relationships, or relationships based on mutual dislike. Overall, 35% of individuals in the studies reported antipathetic relationships, and the presence of these relationships was related to outcomes such as externalizing and internalizing concerns, lower positive regard for others, lower helpful social behavior, victimization and rejection, and lower academic achievement (Card, 2010). In another review, interpersonal sensitivity, or a dispositional concern about negative evaluation, had several negative health outcomes (Marin & Miller, 2013). These included increased risk for infectious diseases and a potentially increased risk for cardiovascular disease. Marin and Miller (2013) also provide evidence that interpersonal sensitivity precedes illness temporally, and that many alternatives have been ruled out, thus suggesting a causal link. Additionally, perceived peer rejection was found to lead to cardiac slowing during the transition to adolescence (i.e., eleven to fourteen years old), and this effect was most pronounced in adolescent girls (Moor, Bos, Crone, & van der Molen, 2013). This effect was not found as strongly among children aged eight to eleven, suggesting a higher sensitivity to peer rejection during adolescence (Moor et al., 2013).

It also appears that perceived rejection informs later responses to peer rejection and acceptance. Neurological fMRI evidence using a simulated social exclusion paradigm suggested that adolescents experiencing firsthand rejection show neural activity relating to distress when seeing another peer accepted later (Masten, Eisenberger, Pfeifer, & Dapretto, 2013). Conversely, rejected adolescents witnessing later peer rejection showed neural activity relating to perspective taking and emotion regulation (Masten et al., 2013).

Plaisier and Konijn (2013) explored the effect of peer rejection on acceptance of antisocial media content and found a relationship between peer rejection, anger, and moral judgment in adolescents. Specifically, it appears that peer rejection creates greater state anger among adolescents, thus leading to moral diminished moral judgments and acceptance of antisocial media content (Plaiser & Konijn, 2013). The relationship between rejection and media choice was not significant among young adults, however (Plaiser & Konijn, 2013). In addition to deviant behaviors, peer rejection appears to play a significant role in adolescent depression. There appears to be a reciprocal relationship between peer rejection and depressive symptoms in the teenage years that forms and preserves unhelpful cycles, although overall results also strongly indicate that peer rejection has some causal influence on negative emotional states (Platt, Kadosh, & Lau, 2013). The researchers suggested from their findings that information-processing and attentional bias strategies may be partly responsible for differences in reactivity to peer rejection among depressed youth (Platt, Kadosh, & Lau, 2013). The authors also discuss new technologies such as neuro-feedback aimed at reducing reactivity to peer rejection by altering underlying cognitive processes (Platt, Kadosh, & Lau, 2013).

Finally, it seems that estimated rejection by others, and not only actual rejection, predicts individual outcomes among adolescents (Zimmer-Gembeck et al., 2013). Specifically, in a sample of Australian adolescents, individuals who over-estimated their own peer rejection from others showed higher rejection sensitivity and felt more victimized, although others did not see them as such (Zimmer-Gembeck et al., 2013). Individuals who under-estimated the degree to which they were rejected were more interpersonally aggressive and their peers saw them that way; however their interpersonal satisfaction was unaffected (Zimmer-Gimbeck et al., 2013). The authors highlight the need to tailor interventions to perceived levels, as well as actual levels, of rejection (Zimmer-Gembeck et al., 2013).

Peer Pressure and Delinquency

The impact of peer pressure and peer influence on adolescent's thoughts, emotions, and behaviors is immense. As mentioned earlier, the drive to affiliate, the need for acceptance, and the fear of rejection characterizing this period of life is a major determinant of current and future functioning (Sigleman & Rider, 2012).

Moreover, it appears that peer influence and pressure impact individuals differently during middle and late adolescence. A longitudinal examination of antisocial adolescents in Pennsylvania and New Mexico suggests that selection (choosing to associate with antisocial peers) and socialization (the effect of deviant peer choices on personal delinquency) processes both impact development of delinquency in middle adolescence (Monahan, Steinberg, & Cauffman, 2009). However, by late adolescence (i.e., sixteen to twenty years old), it appears that personal delinquency is primarily impacted by the socialization processes (Monahan, Steinberg, & Cauffman, 2009). The effect of peer pressure after the age of twenty appears minimal (Monahan, Steinberg, & Cauffman, 2009).

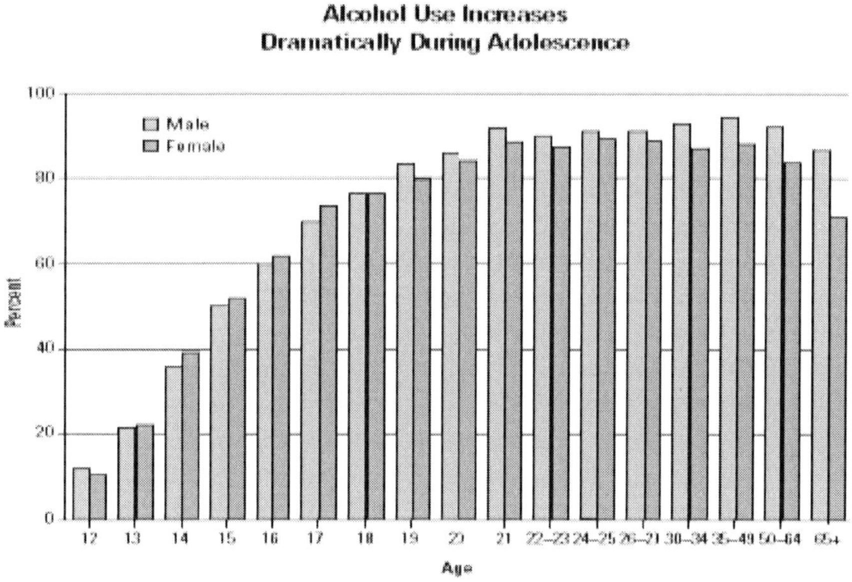

Figure 2.1. Alcohol Use during Adolescence.

Peer pressure impacts the individuals' emotional functioning and relatedness to one-another; however the adolescents' pre-disposition to specific positive or negative emotions may impact their relationships. A preference of attention to positive emotional content seems to be related to avoidance, lower self-sufficiency, and more susceptibility to peer pressure. However, a preference of attention to negative emotional content was related to lower avoidance and more hostility (Buck, Kretsch, & Harden, 2013). These results were lessened for those with premorbid secure attachment styles (Buck, Kretsch, & Harden, 2013). Likewise, the differential need for peer acceptance may relate to differences in individual reward pathways as it appears that peer influence is an important dynamic above and beyond some personality and family factors. This is particularly true in reference to the potential for substance use among this population. Peer use of alcohol during the teenage years predicts use of alcohol during adolescence above and beyond the effect of self-control and parental influence. In a cohort study of over two thousand adolescents surveyed between 2001 and 2010, a relationship between peer use during adolescence and personal use during adolescence was discovered (Visser, de Winter, Veenstra, Verhulst & Reijneveld, 2013). Notably, however, levels of self-control predicted which users would later become abusers (Visser, de Winter, Veenstra, Verhulst & Reijneveld, 2013).

Defensiveness and Pessimism

Many adolescents may adopt defensive or pessimistic demeanors in order to help them navigate the tumultuous waters of interpersonal relationships. In time, these defensive stances have the potential to become longstanding. For example, Sigelman & Rider (2012) note that a healthy attachment to parents often facilitates healthy peer interactions in childhood and adolescence.

Individuals with an insecure style of attachment, or with other extenuating childhood circumstances, may suffer from interpersonal sensitivity in adolescence and early adulthood. This interpersonal sensitivity often leads to defensive attitudes with others such as submission, avoidance, and social inhibition (Marin & Miller, 2013), and these individuals tend to expect negative interactions before they occur. Their experiences are colored by a pessimistic and narrowly focused view of relationships wherein they are attuned to and excessively perceive negative interactions (Marin & Miller, 2013). Maladaptive schemas, such as disconnection, rejection, emotional deprivation, social undesirability, and defectiveness have the potential to develop into a social anxiety disorder or a pervasively avoidant personality disorder (Pinto-Gouveia, Castilho, & Galhardo, 2006; American Psychiatric Association, 2013; Beck, Freeman, & Davis, 2006).

Impression Management

In addition to defensive reactions, adolescents employ a number of other tools in order to manage the way they appear to others. The study of impression management has a long and complex history that deserves brief mention here. Leary and Kowalski (1990) explain the concept and dual-factor theoretical framework through which impression management is viewed. It is seen as the means by which individuals control, or manage, the view of themselves that they present to others, as well as the views that others have of them by extension (Leary & Kowalski, 1990). This process is hypothesized to involve two separate but related parts: impression motivation and impression construction (Leary & Kowalski, 1990).

Impression motivation is the extent to which individuals desire to control their appearance to others and is impacted by an individual's desired end goal and the perceived differences between their actual and ideal image (Leary & Kowalski, 1990). Most impression management appears to occur below the level of conscious awareness, but individuals may, at times, exert conscious efforts to engage in impression management based on their goals (Leary & Kowalski, 1990). Goals may include maintaining self-esteem, social or material outcomes, or developing one's identity (Leary & Kowalski, 1990). Impression construction is the actual process by which individuals construct an image of themselves. This process is hypothesized to be influenced by five components: beliefs about self, wanted and unwanted ideal personalities, actual limitations of options, personal values and public image (Leary & Kowalski, 1990).

Impression management has recently been conceptualized as moralistically bias, which is a component of the construct of social desirability in recent literature (Musch, Ostapczuk, & Klaiber, 2012). This concept is similar to that which is measured by traditional lie scales on tests such as the Minnesota Multiphasic Personality Inventory-2 (MMPI-II) and measures the extent to which one attempts to improve their own image (Musch, Ostapczuk, & Klaiber, 2012). Recent literature has seen the creation and cross-cultural validation of a new measure of social desirability, the Balanced Inventory of Desirable Responding. This measure may replace previous inventories such as the Social Desirability Scale due to its ability to parse out two components of social desirability: impression management/moralistic bias and egoistic bias (Musch, Ostapczuk, & Klaiber, 2012). Egoistic bias can be thought of the extent to which one takes an overly optimistic view of themselves. This type of self-deception is believed to occur below the level of conscious awareness (Musch, Ostapczuk, & Klaiber, 2012).

Thus, impression management may be a strong motivating force at multiple levels. When considering the importance of friendship, peer affiliation, and acceptance as described earlier, it is no wonder that there is a strong incentive for adolescents to present an acceptable version of themselves to the interpersonal world around them.

Physical Development

The changes in physical development during adolescence are largely marked by fast changes in physical and sexual growth known as puberty. Changes during this time include: development of sexual organs, eruption of pubic hair, and growth spurts (Berger, 2005). In addition to phenotype changes, adolescents also begin to experience hormonal changes. The adolescent going through puberty experiences a spike in hormones within the brain in the area known as the hypothalamus. It is in the hypothalamus that changes occur and cause the adolescent to experiences spikes in sexual excitement and sleep patterns, among other changes (Berger, 2005).

Physical Milestones

A major change in the adolescents' physical appearance is that they will likely have a growth spurt in which the adolescent will experience a drastic and immediate change of growth in almost all parts of their body (Berger, 2005). Typically, the growth spurt begins at the extremities, arms and legs, and then transfers to the adolescents' torso, often leaving the adolescents' body appearing disproportionate (Berger, 2005).

The most notable, and possibly most distressing, physical change that occurs is the further development of sexual organs. During puberty, the adolescent boy will experience testicle and penis growth, and scrotum enlargement (Berger, 2005). For adolescent girls, the development of breast occurs and the menstruation cycle begins (Berger, 2005). These changes often induce anxiety and transitions in relationships that the adolescent may not yet be prepared for. The changes in physical appearance for the adolescent often cause increased anxiety and identity concerns that may not have occurred to date.

Values and Identity

Many theorists believe a major milestone of adolescent development is establishing a unique identity and recognizing the values that he or she find most fitting of who they want to be. As discussed earlier in the chapter, Erikson defined the development of identity as the integral process of separating oneself from the family constellation while also holding on to the values that are important to the individual. In understanding these needs for identity it is clear that the adolescent's family plays an important role in the development of values and identity.

Shultheiss and Blustein (1994) completed a study to identify the influence of parent-attachment relationships on identity formation. Results showed a significant relationship between parent-attachment and identity formation among young women, however it did not find a significant relationship between attachment and identity formation of young men (Shultheiss & Blustein, 1994). It is clear that further research needs to be completed to best understand the relationship between parental and adolescent relationships on the development of identity, especially identifying the differences between boys and girls. However impacted the adolescents' attachment to their parents, research shows that the parent child relationship itself has an impact on the development of identity. Quintana and Kerr (1993) studied the impact of interpersonal connectedness with achievement and individuation. Results showed that those students that were able to separate and connect with their parents and peers were more likely to do better in school and have lower rates of psychological distress (Quintana & Kerr, 1993). Having specific types of relationships with adolescents is not as imperative as their ability to separate and connect to others when needed.

Independence and Power Struggles

Adolescence is marked with the need to separate oneself as an individual being, which often leads to power struggles within the adolescent's home and at school. An adolescent might frequently test the boundaries of their rules at home and at school, not because they have malicious intent to damage their familial relationships or to do poorly in school but instead as a way of seeking freedom and independence in their world. Freeman (1994) investigated the relationship of power among a variety of adolescents to identify how power is displayed among a variety of youth. Research showed that a combination of high-achieving school leaders and low-achieving school vandals both rated the desire to have power in their lives as important (Freeman, 1994).

COGNITIVE DEVELOPMENT

As discussed earlier in the chapter, Piaget described a major change in the adolescents' cognitive development in which the adolescent begins to develop abstract reasoning skills. In adolescence, the adolescent is able to analyze and think more logically, however adolescence is often marked with egocentric thinking, in addition to the logical reasoning.

Thinking and Reasoning

Adolescents often struggle with decision-making tactics. In addition to this they struggle with weighing the risks and benefits of specific choices. Adolescents' prefrontal lobes, the part of the brain responsible for decision making, are not fully developed, which often leads to risky decision making. In many instances, adolescents might worry about potential disaster and over-analyze a decision. For many, the rush of making risky and callus decisions lead to further excitement (Berger, 2005). Considering the social aspects of adolescent decision-making, often the more dangerous or risky behaviors (i.e., driving fast or ditching class) are often regarded highly among peers and gain respect among classmates. In developing decision-making skills with adolescents, it is important that time and assistance is provided to further expand rationalism. Adolescents need more time for their brain to develop and assistance in helping them think of possibilities that they might not have thought of regarding risky behaviors.

Information Processing and Abstract Thinking

A hallmark of adolescent cognitive development is that the adolescent is able to develop possible scenarios to a situation and not just think about realities. This type of thinking is called hypothetical thought and it allows the adolescent to think about complicated issues and begin reasoning with possible realities. Adolescents, unlike children, are able to think about alternatives to their reality, thus leading to prompting change or criticizing the current reality.

Along with hypothetical thinking, the adolescent is able to think of an idea and draw possibilities from it. This is known as using deductive reasoning. Adolescents become able to identify and infer what something might be like due to past knowledge and experiences. This is something that they were not capable of prior to this age range.

Concrete Thinking

We know from the readings earlier in the chapter that Piaget described new logical thinking such as formal operational thought. This form of thinking allows the adolescent to draw conclusions from hypothetical scenarios and not strictly from personal experiences. However, a large portion of adolescent thinking is surrounded by personal concerns and individual beliefs.

Adolescent Egocentrism

During this time the adolescent often thinks of him or herself frequently and is concerned with how others perceive him or her. However, the adolescent often thinks of him or herself at an inflated level and excludes others, leading to adolescent egocentrism. The adolescent will use his or her skills to hypothesize what another person might be thinking. However, instead of accepting that as a possible thought, the adolescent accepts those beliefs as a fact, often leading to false conclusions about others (Berger, 2005). For example, if a close friend of the adolescent does not say hello to them in the hallway at school, the adolescent might believe their friend is angry with them and infer that "no one likes me."

Another aspect of the egocentric thought is that the adolescent may believe that they are incapable of being harmed, which is known as the invincibility fable (Berger, 2005). It is because of this thinking that adolescents often act in reckless ways due to the belief that they will not suffer from any consequences, whether it be physically harmful or getting in trouble with the law.

Often adolescents believe that they are being observed or that other people are largely interested in what they are engaging in which is known as the imaginary audience (Berger, 2005). The adolescent might begin to hypothesize how others would react to changes within themselves often leading to sadness or anger if they are not recognized in the manner expected.

In understanding adolescent egocentric thought, it is important to identify that the adolescent is struggling with social needs, and they are struggling to find their place in the world. This is often why adolescents put great effort into their looks and the importance of their peer relationships.

Moral Beliefs and Spiritual Values

The moral and spiritual beliefs of adolescents often play a large role in their interpersonal decision making and behavior. Sigelman and Rider (2012) highlight adolescence as a time of crucial moral development. This period is viewed as the beginning of conventional moral reasoning during which fairness, legitimate authority, and earning social approval become of primary importance (Sigelman & Rider, 2012). Some adolescents begin to internalize principles of social justice as well (Sigelman & Rider, 2012). Additionally, the desire to become a moral person becomes a goal toward which adolescents begin to strive (Sigelman & Rider, 2012).

Many adolescents, however, lack mature moral reasoning abilities, moral emotional abilities, or adequate social information processing skills, and subsequently choose criminal activity rather than moral behavior (Sigelman & Rider, 2012). When describing this process, the authors highlight previous research on social information-processing suggesting that aggressive adolescents show deficient and biased processing at all stages. This includes encoding of primarily hostile cues in a situation, interpretation of hostile intent, plans to retaliate, generating only aggressive options, weighing advantages of aggressive behavior favorably, and acting out as a result (Sigelman & Rider, 2012). Clearly, the moral beliefs and practices of adolescents will have an important impact on the other individuals with whom they interact. Indeed, Sigelman and Rider (2012) cite literature suggesting that peer groups are formed in high school based on similar behaviors and labels. Additionally, group membership in high school predicts later behavior (Sigelman, 2012). A theory described by Gerald Patterson posits that removal from coercive environments may even be a primary means to change patterns of criminal behavior among adolescents (Sigelman & Rider, 2012). Clearly, moral decision making abilities and interpersonal decision making are interconnected.

In a related vein, spiritual beliefs, values, and development are also bi-directionally related to interpersonal dynamics in adolescence. Walker and Reimer (2006) outline the relationship between moral and spiritual development among adolescents, noting that morality and spirituality are often not distinct domains in real life, and people often invoke religion and spirituality while handling moral issues (Walker & Reimer, 2006). Verma and Sta. Maria (2006) highlighted the changing dynamics of adolescent spiritual development. The authors remarked that diverse cultural changes have large effects on spiritual development, including macro-societal trends, changes in family structure and relations, and peer and school relationships (Verma & Sta. Maria, 2006). Specific changes noted include the lack of familial, spiritual direction due to decreasing family sizes, impairment of spiritual socialization due to family mobility, increases in peer groups without normative moral or spiritual values, and use of information and communication technologies to spiritually connect with peers around the world (Verma & Sta. Maria, 2006). Clearly, the spiritual and religious domain of life is affected by changing global interpersonal dynamics among adolescents.

The clinical areas of identity development, attachment, and spiritual thriving are other areas that highlight the interpersonal nature of spiritual and religious development. Two pathways through which spiritual identities can develop include collective and personal identities (Templeton & Eccles, 2006). Additionally, the need for connection is one of the primary foundations provided for the development of a spiritual identity in adolescence (Templeton & Eccles, 2006). Moreover, both insecure and secure attachment styles have been related to the search for connectedness in spirituality (Granqvist & Dickie, 2006). This search for spirituality is posited to occur through different mechanisms, however, for those with different attachment styles. For those with a childhood and adolescent insecure attachment style, the search for God is compensatory – making up for what was lacking (Granqvist & Dickie, 2006). For those with secure attachment patterns, the search is one of correspondence – searching for an image of God that matches the image of the parents. The authors cite evidence that indeed suggests that those with secure attachment styles at a younger age form similar emotional relationships with God and with later romantic partners (Granqvist & Dickie, 2006). Moreover, religion and spirituality are empirically supported as means of thriving in multiple domains for adolescents, including personal health, academic achievement, civic engagement, and altruism toward others (King & Benson, 2006). Clearly, there are important ties between interpersonal and religious and spiritual components of life in multiple domains.

Finally, given burgeoning literature on the interrelationships between interpersonal functioning and spiritual and moral development among adolescents, it is no surprise that the influence of peer and nonparent influences on spiritual development has been avidly explored. Schwartz, Bukowski, and Aoki (2006) present a summary of literature in this area. Some themes that emerge include the importance of mentors, the importance of friendships, and the importance of spiritual directors as a context for spiritual direction (Schwartz, Bukowski, & Aoki, 2006). Mentoring was related to a variety of decreased risk factors and increased protective factors during adolescence. These included decreased drug use, increased resilience, increased academic performance, better interpersonal relationships, and a supportive relationship (Schwartz, Bukowski, & Aoki, 2006). The authors further conceptualize friendship as a model for spirituality by describing its transcendent relational quality, link with goodness, and focus on deep interpersonal knowledge. The authors emphasize that, just as friendship contributes to spirituality/religion, spirituality/religion also contributes to friendship (Schwartz, Bukowski, & Aoki, 2006). Finally, the authors examined evidence suggesting that positive relationships with youth ministers (church) led to numerous positive outcomes for adolescents, such as a sense of moral responsibility, personal relationship with God, hopeful and positive attitudes, and engagement with mission and service (Schwartz, Bukowski, & Aoki, 2006). The examples and ideas presented here provide strong evidence that spiritual, religious, moral, and interpersonal domains are all strong interconnected forces in adolescence.

Academic Development

There are many factors that contribute to and deter from academic development. In understanding how peer relationships impact the adolescent, it is important to note that it is important for their academic development as well. Supportive interactions among students and teachers lead to improved academic development and improved cognitive abilities. Also, having a structured home life and supportive parents lead to better academic outcomes (Berger, 2005).

Achievements

Largely when academic achievement is discussed, it is likely split into separate categories of over-achievement and under-achievement. Farquhar and Payne (1964) define over-achievement as a person who "exceeds an aptitude-base expectancy of academic performance" (p. 874). Whereas, an adolescent who under-achieves "falls below his [or her] expected performance" (Farquhar & Payne, 1964, p. 874). So what causes an adolescent to under-achieve? There is not simply one factor that contributes to under-achievement; it is a variety of issues that provide academic under-achievement including: alienation from school, experiencing bullying, behavioral needs, and parental factors.

Alienation from School

During adolescence, many young people feel separated from their school and society in itself. Warner and Hanson (1970) described the misconception that feeling alienated from school was an individual issue and was due to maladaptive behaviors. The authors described alienation as a societal issue and something that can occur due to race, sex, socio-economic status, and a variety of other factors (Warner & Hanson, 1970). The formulation of the educational structure appears to be a factor in adolescent alienation as it is made to emulate traditional society. However, during adolescence, a time when an individual is attempting to define him or herself as an autonomous person, there may be a disconnect from how they see themselves and how others' perceive them (Warner & Hanson, 1970). The educational structure warrants adolescent independence, however they must also must meet the demands and goals that are in opposition of their autonomy (Warner & Hanson, 1970). In relation to academic needs, often the persistent force of academic success is placed upon these students. For those students who are struggling, it will only lead to further alienation and further academic underachievement (Warner & Hanson, 1970).

Bullying and School Attitude

Bullying is a major issue among today's adolescents. Bullying can occur in a variety of formats and a multitude of manners that all can have damaging effects on the adolescent. In a study by Espelage, Bosworth and Simon (2000) findings showed that over eighty-percent of adolescents had experienced some form of bullying in their lives. Often, many adolescents experience harassment from their peers for years on end. Bullying can include attempts to injure or insult someone and the purposeful exclusion of an individual from a group (Crothers & Levinson, 2004). Considering the tremendous importance of social needs and peer influence among adolescents, school bullying has a major impact on the adolescent's functioning.

Bullying and the Internet

With the development of the Internet, adolescents now have a multitude of ways to connect to one-another and to further develop their academic efforts. However, there are many risk factors for adolescents who frequent the internet. Internet harassment is a new occurrence in modern society and greatly contributes to adolescent struggles. Often, adolescents will either experience internet bullying, in which a peer or other person might call the adolescent names or threaten him or her over the internet, or victimization, in which the adolescent is sought out by another person and convinced to engage in potentially dangerous or sexual acts (Burrow-Sanchez et al., 2009). Adolescents who are more likely to be a victim of internet harassment typically have less parental control and involvement over internet accessibility (Burrow-Sanchez et al., 2009). In many cases, the parent does not have as much understanding of what is available via the internet; thus it is not being monitored heavily (Burrow-Sanchez et al., 2009). Also, many parents lack the knowledge or comfort to discuss potential concerns with their adolescent (Burrow-Sanchez et al., 2009). Parents may perceive a conversation with their teen as constructive and useful, while the adolescent does not see benefit in the communication (Burrow-Sanchez et al., 2009). As a provider, providing information to the parents to best assist with mediation of internet use along with appropriate amounts of adolescent control is an important step in reduction of online victimization. Also, providing psychoeducational therapies to adolescents about online victimization can solicit open communication and prevention.

Behavioral Problems

Adolescence is marked by periods of biological, social and familial changes. During these transitioning years, it is common for these young people to act out and engage in risky behaviors that lead to behavioral problems. We know that even though adolescents are able to think more abstractly that ever before in their life, they are also prone to risky decision-making and behavioral problems.

Many adolescents report high levels of stress during this transition period, which may lead to maladaptive coping skills and further psychiatric issues. Adolescent girls are highly susceptible for anxiety disorders and both males and females run the risk of developing depression (Berger, 2005). In many cases, these young people develop eating disorders or act-out against adults

(Berger, 2005). In working with adolescents it is important to understand the underlying causes of the maladaptive behaviors.

Parental Involvement

The impact of social relationships and family relationships on academic development is vast. Baskin, Quintana and Slaten (2013) completed a study to identify the impact of psychological distress and peer relationships on the adolescent individual. What was found is that those adolescents who experienced more psychological distress were more likely to do poorly in school (Baskin, Quintana & Slaten, 2013). Negative peer relationships and family distress leads to lower academic achievement. For adolescents, having a structured home life and consistent, supportive friends allow room for flourishing academic achievement.

A study completed on the impact of family on young African American males showed less impact of the specific parenting characteristics on the young male's academic achievement; however it did describe the impact of having two parents within the home (Hines & McCoy, 2012). Those young men who had two adult parents in their home had higher academic achievement (Hines &McCoy, 2012). What we can infer from this is that the father's role in the young man's life is tremendously impactful on not only the adolescents' psychological functioning, but also his academic functioning. Hines and McCoy (2012) also found other factors impacted improved academic functioning, such as the parent's educational level and the parents' academic expectations of the adolescent. Those adolescents that had parents who expected the adolescent to achieve good grades and excel in academic work actually did better in school as a result.

The parents' role in the adolescents' life also has implications for how the adolescent will develop an understanding of his/her environment and how they manage their time academically. Trusty and Lampe (1997) completed research of parental involvement and the type of locus of control the adolescent perceives on their life. Research shows that those individuals who had parents highly involved in their life appeared to have a higher locus of control over their life, thus resulting in improved schoolwork and higher academic achievement (Trusty & Lampe, 1997).

Research has shown that there could be gender differences in academic achievement between adolescent boys and girls. Christopher (1967) identified the importance of parent-child relationships and parental values on adolescents' academic achievements. Research showed that for males the relationship with their parent was less important than the parental values, identifying that even if the parent-child relationship is strained the values continue (Christopher, 1967). However, with adolescent females, there was a significant importance of the relationship on academic successes in addition to the importance of family values (Christopher, 1967).

Case Scenario 2.1.

James

James is a 17-year-old Hispanic male who is beginning to fail in his grades at school. His parents report that he is becoming defiant at home and does not appear to listen to the rules set-forth. James will often "talk back" to his parents or tell them that he does not have to follow their rules. James' teachers state that he is quiet in school and does not offer much in his responses to their questions posed to the class, however he does appear to listen during his classes. James has always been a straight-A student and has never had issues in his classes until recently. There are no major shifts in his family dynamics per his parent's report and his teachers cannot find a reason why James appears to be struggling. James is the youngest of three boys and often gets into fights with his brothers in his home. James' brothers often complain that James is "too sensitive" and that he is "weird" for not having a girlfriend yet. James began two counseling sessions with a guidance counselor in school and has stated he dislikes his brothers. James does not speak much in his counseling sessions and states at times "this therapy stuff is dumb."

IMPLICATIONS FOR PROVIDERS ADOLESCENTS

Given the ethical mandate to practice competently concerning those with whom providers work, it is imperative that practitioners take the time to consider the impact of these findings for their work (American Psychological Association, 2010a). Certainly, each of these areas of interpersonal functioning and dynamics offer important insight for clinical practice.

When considering research on peer affiliation, it is clear that its overall impact on adolescent development is very important. It is common for providers to conceptualize adolescents through the lens of attachment theory and family systemic approaches, such that the role of the family becomes primary in the understanding of the adolescent. However, research indicated here has noted the powerful effect of peer group status, perceived social acceptance, and friendship in various domains such as mental health and risk behaviors (Sigelman & Rider, 2012). Thus, it is important for providers to gain a thorough understanding of both an adolescent's actual and perceived peer relationship functioning in order to gain a thorough understanding of their presenting problem.

In terms of rejection and acceptance, it is clear that peer rejection has a number of tangible consequences that extend beyond interpersonal domains (Sigelman & Rider, 2012). These consequences, as mentioned earlier, may be neurological or medical in nature. This suggests the powerful overall effect of peer rejection and acceptance. The importance of acceptance may be especially pronounced in girls as mentioned earlier (Sigelman & Rider, 2012). However, in creating interventions, rejection is an important variable to consider, whether it be perceived or estimated rejection or actual rejection (Sigelman & Rider, 2012). Thus, it will be important for providers to gain an adolescent's perspective on the extent to which they feel rejected or accepted by others and to assess behavioral indicators of these variables. This finding may also suggest the usefulness of cognitive re-framing strategies for adolescents who struggle with perceived acceptance or rejection (Hanna, Hanna & Keys, 1999). Finally, research presented here suggests the importance of a thorough medical history to check for any physical indicators of psychological phenomena (Berger, 2005).

Clearly peer pressure is also an important influence on the lives of adolescents above and beyond some family factors (Sigelman & Rider, 2012). However, the importance of attachment style in predicting peer attachment patterns is also highlighted here (Baskin, Quintana & Slaten, 2013). This may aid providers in making predictions about which children are likely to struggle with peer pressure and help prepare parents proactively by obtaining useful and effective resources and knowledge. Also, research on deviant friend selection vs. socialization may inform treatment targets among adolescents of different age groups (Sigelman & Rider, 2012).

In terms of defensiveness and pessimism, this chapter aids providers in understanding social anxiety and avoidant personality styles from a broader developmental perspective (Marin & Miller, 2013). Movement past diagnostic criteria into a more holistic conceptualization of adolescent development assists providers in assessing idiosyncratic components of experience (Marin & Miller, 2013). For example, providers have the opportunity to explore the extent to which a socially anxious teenager may feel pessimistic about their ability to interact with others in order to assess possible developmental pathways by which this pessimism may have developed (e.g., poor attachment, poor early peer relations, etc.).

Research on impression motivation, impression construction and impression management behaviors in adolescence helps break down the reasons and means by which adolescents may control their appearance toward others (Leary & Kowalski, 1990). If impression management is conceptualized as a type of defensiveness, then validating and empathizing with adolescents efforts to protect themselves or improve their image may be a helpful strategy to connect with them (Leary & Kowalski, 1990). An understanding of various components of impression management strategies, then, gives providers an opportunity to understand this behavior and help adolescents choose productive and healthy relational strategies.

The dynamics of friendship choice and group identity formation also become more complex during adolescence, as mentioned earlier (Sigelman & Rider, 2012). If providers are able to understand the processes by which friends and groups are formed, they can more competently assess normative vs. pathological interpersonal behaviors. Providers may also be able to better assist parents in recognizing deviant vs. normal teenage behavior. Finally, providers may better be able to plan interventions and have conversations with adolescents that reflect their current stage of group identity formation. The extent to which adolescents engage in homophily in their group identities is also important, and may be a target of intervention if it prevents them from having diverse relational experiences (Sigelman & Rider, 2012).

Finally, this chapter highlights the interrelatedness of interpersonal functioning and spiritual/religious and moral domains. Although spiritual and religious functioning and history should constitute a regular part of clinical assessment, specific questions exploring the interconnectedness of interpersonal and spiritual/religious/moral domains are suggested through the research explored here (Sigelman & Rider, 2012). These include assessment of group moral decision making, familial and peer spiritual values, community religious involvement, and other important areas. An understanding of the impact of religion and spirituality in the interpersonal lives of adolescents help providers practice more competently and take a more integrated perspective of the whole individual (Sigelman & Rider, 2012). Finally, for those providers practicing from a religiously integrative perspective, the present volume presents areas for specific intervention.

CLINICAL REVIEW OF CASE

The case of James presented in this chapter provides a number of issues regarding possible developmental changes that James may be experiencing leading to a reduction of academic success. First, James is at a pivotal point in his life when his hormones are surging and he is experiencing major biological changes. As a result, often many young person's often become more irritable and on edge with their families. His parents would benefit with further understanding the changes he is experiencing in order better understand the changes in James' emotions. Also, the relationship with his brothers appear to be strained, possibly due to the emotional changes James is experiencing due to his developmental changes, which is causing a discord in the home. If James were able to better understand how his emotional changes are normal he may feel less at odds with his brothers in the home. Also, it important to understand James' action in school as it appears he is not active during his classes. Hypoactivity is a common symptom of depression, and in understanding how developmental changes can cause depression in adolescence, early interventions for preventing major symptoms of depression for James can lead to improved outcomes for reducing psychological distress later in life.

Also, there are a variety of other factors the competent provider should be aware of. First, James is Hispanic and developing an understanding of how the family communicates specifically considering his cultural framework is important to better understand James' relationship with his parents. Additionally, in understanding how academic achievement can be impacted by bullying, the providers for James should accurately identify if he is experiencing bullying in school or if his relationship with his older brothers is leading to distress. James may be failing school due to bullying behaviors he is experiencing from his brothers. Lastly, are the biological changes James is undergoing causing significant distress on James' life so much so that he is unable to focus in school? These are issues and questions that the providers and adults working with James should be asking. Review the knowledge you have gained in this chapter by answering the questions in Exercise 2. 1 *Review*.

Exercise 2.1. Understanding Developmental Changes

1. What is the psychosocial stage that Erikson described occurs through adolescence and what are the overlying issues that occur in this stage? How does this compare to Piaget's stages and Mahler's stages?

2. What are some strategies that a provider can employ to work with a defiant juvenile justice involved adolescent client?
3. Describe three physical changes that occur during adolescence and how does this impact their emotional functioning?
4. What are major emotional changes that the adolescent is experiencing and what are the causes of these changes?
5. Describe forms of bullying that occur during adolescence and identify ways that this impacts the adolescents' academic functioning.
6. Briefly describe the importance of the relationship of the adolescents' peers during this stage in the young persons' life. What are some changes in social relationships that may relate to juvenile delinquency?
7. Name and describe three changes in cognitive thinking that occur during adolescence. How are these changes related to cognitive distortions and criminal thinking errors often witnessed in juvenile justice involved adolescents?

CONCLUSION

It is evident that the development and functioning of adolescents is complex, and the issues and examples are as diverse as the individuals themselves. Although research continues in this area, a growing awareness of some of the relevant topics that providers will discuss with adolescences is crucial. In order to become aware of these areas, it is important that providers continue to explore the existing pool of research. Nonetheless, perhaps much of the expertise gained by providers will come from the actual work of helping adolescents through the teenage years. A degree of inquisitiveness and curiosity toward the experiences of each individual is also necessary. The field of behavioral health offers important tools and strategies to assist with developmental transitions, as well as the problems that arise during this period. Coupled with sensitivity to ideographic and normative adolescent experiences, much good can be done.

Walk Away Points

- Emotional upheaval is likely to occur in adolescence, however hormones are not the only factor to the change of emotions.

Anxiety and depression can be increased due to the biological and social/interpersonal changes that occur during adolescence.

- Many adolescents experience disproportionate rage and as a provider working with these adolescents it is imperative to be skilled in manners of relating to the adolescent and to assist them with developing appropriate coping skills. These adolescents run the risk of acting out behaviors that may lead to future consequences.
- Peer relationships highly impact the interpersonal functioning of the adolescent. The adolescent is motivated by peer pressure, avoiding rejection, and the impressions of their peers.
- Adolescence is marked by the physical changes of puberty. The adolescent begins to experience changes in sexual organs, overall growth of the body, and other physical changes. These changes often lead to distress and anxiety within the adolescent.
- The adolescent now begins to think of what morals they find important and separate themselves from the morals that they do not find valuable. These morals are often influenced by their spiritual beliefs, which are often beginning to adjust and change at this age.
- The adolescent is now able to think abstractly about hypothetical situations and conjure possible scenarios to actions. It is a this age that the adolescents' cognitive develop now becomes more abstract.
- Academic needs in adolescence are often impacted by social and familial relationships. Teens are now experiencing issues related to bullying and alienation from peers/school at higher rates than ever. Parent-child relationships can have a significant impact on academic achievement.

References

American Psychiatric Association (2013). *Diagnostic and statistical manual of mental disorders, fifth edition (DSM-5)*. Washington, DC: Author (ISBN 978-0-89042-554-1).

American Psychological Association. (2010a). *Ethical principles of psychologists and code of conduct* (2002, amended June 1, 2010). Retrieved from http://www.apa.org/ethics/code/index.aspx.

Baskin T. W., Quintana S. M., & Slaten C. D. (2013) Family belongingness, gang friendships, and psychological distress in adolescent achievement.

Journal of Counseling & Development 92 DOI: 10.1002/j.1556-6676.2014.00166.x.

Beck, A., & Freeman, A., & Davis, D. (2006). *Cognitive therapy of personality disorders* (2nd ed). New York: Guilford Press.

Berger, K.S. (2005). *The developing person: Through the life span* (6th ed). New York: Worth Publishers.

Brown, B.B. & Lohr, M. J. (1987). Peer-group affiliation and adolescent self-esteem: An integration of Ego-identity and symbolic-interaction theories. *Journal of Personality and Social Psychology*, 52(1), 47-55.

Buck, K. A.; Kretsch, N. & Harden, K. P. (2013). Positive attentional bias, attachment style, and susceptibility to peer influence. *Journal of Research on Adolescence*, 23(4), 605-613.

Burrow-Sanchez, J. J.; Call, M. E.; Zheng, R.; & Drew, C. J. (2009). How school providers can help prevent online victimization. *Journal of Counseling & Development*. 89, 3-11.

Card, N. A. (2010). Antipathetic relationships in child and adolescent development: A meta-analytic review and recommendations for an emerging area of study. *Developmental Psychology*, 46(2), 516-529.

Christopher, S. A. (1967). Parental relationship and value orientation as factors in academic achievement. *Personnel and Guidance Journal*. 921-926.

Crothers, L. M. & Levinson, E. M. (2004). Assessment of bullying: A review of methods and instruments. *Journal of Counseling & Development*. 83, 496-503.

Currarini, S.; Jackson, M. O.; & Pin, P. (2010). Identifying the roles of race-based choice and chance in high school friendship network formation. *Proceedings of the National Academy of Sciences (PNAS)*, 107(11), 4857-4861.

Erford, B. T.; Erford, B. M.; Lattanzi, G.; Weller, J.; Schein, H.; Wolf, E.; Hughes, M.; Darrow, J.; Savin-Murphy, J.; & Peacock, E. (2011). Counseling outcomes from 1990 to 2008 for school-age youth with depression: A meta-analysis. *Journal of Counseling & Development*. 89, 439-457.

Erikson, E. H. (1968). Identity, youth, and crisis. New York: Norton.

Espelage, D. L.; Bosworth, K.; & Simon, T. R. (2000). Examining the social context of bullying behaviors in early adolescence. *Journal of Counseling & Development*, 78, 326-434.

Freeman, B. (1994). Power motivation and youth: An analysis of troubled students and student leaders. *Journal of Counseling & Development*. 72, 661-671.

Dixon A. L., Scheidegger C., & McWhirter J. J. (2009). The adolescent mattering experience: Gender variations in perceived mattering, anxiety, and depression. *Journal of Counseling & Development,* 87, 302-310.

Dolcini, M. M. & Adler, N. E. (1994). Perceived competencies, peer group affiliation, and risk behavior among early adolescents. *Health Psychology*, 13(6), 496-506.

Fujimoto, K. & Valente, T. W. (2013). Alcohol peer influence of participating in organized school activities: A network approach. *Health Psychology*, 32(10), 1084-1092.

Granqvist, P. & Dickie, J. R. (2006). Attachment and spiritual development in childhood and adolescence. In Roehlkepartian, E. C.; King, P. E.; Wagener, L. & Benson, P. L. (Eds.) *The Handbook of spiritual development* (pp. 124-136). Thousand Oaks, CA: Sage Publications.

Hanna, F. J.; Hanna, C. A. & Keys, S. G. (1999). Fifty strategies for counseling defiant, aggressive adolescents: Reaching, accepting, and relating. *Journal of Counseling and Development.* 77, 395-405.

Hains, A. A. (1992). Comparison of cognitive-behavioral stress management techniques with adolescent boys. *Journal of Counseling & Development.* 20, 600-606.

Hamachek, D. E. (1985) The self's development and ego growth: Conceptual analysis and implications for providers. *Journal of Counseling and Development*, 64. 136-142.

Hines E. M. & McCoy C. H. (2012). Parental characteristics, ecological factors, and the academic achievement of African American males. *Journal of Counseling & Development.* 91.

Hoare, C. (1991). Psychosocial identity development and cultural others. *Journal of Counseling and Development*, 70. 45-53.

Inhelder, B. & Piaget, J. (1958). *The growth of logical thinking from childhood to adolescence.* New York: Basic Books.

Ivy, A. E.& Goncalves, O. F. (1988). Developmental therapy: Integrating developmental processes into the clinical practice. *Journal of Counseling and Development*, 66. 406-413.

Jacobs, J. E., Lanza, S., Osgood, D. W., Eccles, J. S., & Wigfield, A. (2002). Changes in children's self-competence and values: Gender and domain differences across grades one through twelve. *Child Development,* 73, 509-527.

King, P. E. & Benson, P. L. (2006). Spiritual development and adolescent well-being and thriving. In Roehlkepartian, E. C.; King, P. E.; Wagener,

L. & Benson, P. L. (Eds.) *The Handbook of spiritual development* (pp. 124-136). Thousand Oaks, CA: Sage Publications.

Leary, M. R. & Kowalski, R. M. (1990). Impression management: A literature review and two-component model. *Psychological Bulletin*, 107(1), 34-47.

Mahler, M. S., Pine, Fred, Bergman (1975). *The psychological birth of the human infant: Symbiosis and individuation.* New York: Basic Books.

Marin, T. J. & Miller, G. E. (2013). The interpersonally sensitive disposition and health: An integrative review. *Psychological Bulletin*, 139(5), 941-984.

Masten, C. L.; Eisenberger, N. I.; Pfeifer, J. H. & Dapretto, M. (2013). Neural responses to witnessing peer rejection after being socially excluded: fMRI as a window into adolescents' emotional processing. *Developmental Science*, 16(5), 743-759.

Miller, L. D.; Short, C.; Garland, E. J.; & Clark, S. (2010). The ABCs of CBT (Cognitive Behavior Therapy): Evidence-based approaches to child anxiety in public school settings. Journal of Counseling & Development. 88, 432-39

Monahan, K. C.; Steinberg, L. & Cauffman, E. (2009). Affiliation with antisocial peers, susceptibility to peer influence, and antisocial behavior during the transition to adulthood. *Developmental Psychology*, 45(6), 1520-1530.

Moor, B. G.; Bos, M. G. N.; Crone, E. A. & van der Molen, M. W. (2013). Peer rejection cues induce cardiac slowing after transition into adolescence.

Musch, J.; Ostapczuk, M. & Klaiber, Y. (2012). Validating an inventory for the assessment of egoistic bias and moralistic bias as two separable components of social desirability. *Journal of Personality Assessment*, 94(6), 620-629.

Pinto-Gouveia, J., Castilho, P. & Galhardo, A. (2006). Early maladaptive schemas and social phobia. Cognitive Therapy and Research, 30, 571-584.

Plaisier, X. S. & Konijn, E. A. (2013). Rejected by peers – attracted to antisocial media content: Rejection-based anger impairs moral judgment among adolescents. *Developmental Psychology*, 49(6), 1165-1173.

Platt, B.; Kadosh, K. C. & Lau, J. Y. F. (2013). The role of peer rejection in adolescent depression. *Depression and Anxiety*, 30, 809-821.

Quintana, S. M. & Kerr, J. (1993) Relational needs in late adolescent separation-individuation. *Journal of Counseling & Development.* 71, 349-354.

Reilly, J. (2014, December 17). *Daily Mail.* Retrieved December 27, 2014, from Daily Mail News: http://www.dailymail.co.uk/news/article-2877873/Teen-charged-alleged-rape-16-year-old-girl-attacked-photos-naked-body-posted-social-media.html.

Rusby, J. C.; Westling, E.; Crowley, R. & Light, J. M. (2013). Concurrent and predictive associations between early adolescent perceptions of peer affiliates and mood states collected in real time via ecological momentary assessment methodology. *Psychological Assessment*, 25(1), 47-60.

Segev, R.; Shoham, A. & Ruvio, A. (2013). Gift giving among adolescents: Exploring motives, the effects of givers' personal characteristics and the use of impression management tactics. *Journal of Consumer Marketing*, 30(5), 436-449.

Shultheiss, D. P. & Blustein D. L. (1994). Contributions of family relationship factors to the identity formation process. *Journal of Counseling & Development*. 73, 159-166.

Sigelman, C. K. & Rider, E. A. (2012). Life-span Human Development (7e). Belmont, CA: Wadsworth Cengage.

Schwartz, K. D.; Bukowski, W. M.; & Aoki, W. T. (2006). Mentors, friends, and gurus: Peer and nonparent influences on spiritual development. In Roehlkepartian, E. C.; King, P. E.; Wagener, L. & Benson, P. L. (Eds.) *The Handbook of spiritual development* (pp. 124-136). Thousand Oaks, CA: Sage Publications.

Templeton, J. L. & Eccles, J. S. (2006). The relation between spiritual development and identity process. In Roehlkepartian, E. C.; King, P. E.; Wagener, L. & Benson, P. L. (Eds.) *The Handbook of spiritual development* (pp. 124-136). Thousand Oaks, CA: Sage Publications.

Trusty, J. & Lampe R. E. (1997). Relationship of high-school seniors' perceptions of parental involvement and control to seniors' locus of control. *Journal of Counseling and Development*. 75, 375-385.

U.S. Department of Health and Human Services. (1999). *Mental health: A report of the Surgeon General.* Rockville, MD: Author.

Verma, S. & Sta. Maria, M. (2006). The changing global context of adolescent spirituality. In Roehlkepartian, E. C.; King, P. E.; Wagener, L. & Benson, P. L. (Eds.) *The Handbook of spiritual development* (pp. 124-136). Thousand Oaks, CA: Sage Publications.

Visser, L.; de Winter, A. F.; Veenstra, R.; Verhulst, F. C. & Reijneveld, S. A. (2013). Alcohol use and abuse in young adulthood: Do self-control and parents' perceptions of friends during adolescence modify peer influence? The TRAILS study. *Addictive Behaviors*, 38, 2841-2846.

Walker, L. J. & Reimer, K. S. (2006). The relationship between moral and spiritual development. In Roehlkepartian, E. C.; King, P. E.; Wagener, L. & Benson, P. L. (Eds.) *The Handbook of spiritual development* (pp. 124-136). Thousand Oaks, CA: Sage Publications.

Warner and Hanson (1970). Alienated youth: The provider‘s task. *Personnel and Guidance Journal*. 48 (6), 443-449.

Zimmer-Gembeck, M. J.; Nesdale, D.; McGregor, L.; Mastro, S.; Goodwin, B. & Downey, G. (2013). Comparing reports of peer rejection: Associations with rejection sensitivity, victimization, aggression, and friendship. *Journal of Adolescence*, 36, 1237-1246.

BIOGRAPHICAL SKETCH

Lee A. Underwood, PsyD.

Dr. Underwood is a Licensed Clinical Psychologist in several states and Certified Sex Offender Treatment Provider (CSOTP) and is affiliated with egent University School of Psychology and Counseling in Virginia Beach, Virginia Youth Development Institute (YDI) in Phoenix, Arizona. He has served as an Executive Clinical Officer for several large residential treatment, juvenile justice and criminal justice programs for adolescents and adults with sex offending, severe mental health, co-occurring mental health and substance use disorders, substance use, trauma and disruptive behavioral disorders. Dr. Underwood is nationally renowned specialist in the area of juvenile sex offender formation. As Director of the Center for Addictions and Offender Research operated by Regent University, he and his research team at Regent are responsible for most of the cutting edge research taking place in this arena; his work is constantly cited by others working in this area. Dr. Underwood has worked extensively with residential and juvenile justice programs and has been recognized by the Office of Juvenile Justice and Delinquency Prevention (OJJDP), American Institutes for Research (AIR) and the Substance Abuse & Mental Health Services Administration (SAMSHA) as one of the leading program innovators for juvenile justice and community treatment programs. Dr. Underwood has held a number of policy oriented research, academic, clinical and consulting positions over his career with federal, state and private agencies for research, program design, development, implementation and evaluation of services. He has published over 50 peer reviewed journal articles and 17 treatment manuals on sex offending, mental health, substance use, trauma needs of females, forensic and cultural needs of persons involved in the juvenile justice and mental health systems as means of distributing the findings of his research. His most recent books include *Counseling Adolescents Competently* (in final production by Sage Publishers) and *Adolescents in Conflic*t (Taylor Made Publishing).

Frances L. L. Dailey, PhD.

Dr. Frances Dailey is a Professional Counselor and Executive Director of Dailey Consulting and has published over 10 professional journal articles. She serves as the Project Director for USA Consulting Group, a research and evaluation organization. She teaches Masters students in Community Mental Health Counseling and Forensic Psychology programs. She received her Master's in Counseling from Regent University, School of Psychology and Counseling and her doctorate from Regent University in Counselor Education and Supervision. She is the author of *Adolescents in Crisis: Understanding the Back-story* and author of *Counseling Adolescents Competently* and is involved in several statewide program evaluations for juveniles involved in the juvenile justice system. Her research and clinical interests have focused on survivors of sex trafficking, juveniles in secure care and residential treatment facilities, first generation college students, supervision and multicultural competencies, program design, evaluation and implementation. Her most recent works include program evaluation (of Louisiana's Juvenile Sexual Problem Behavior Program for the United States Office of Juvenile Justice and Delinquency Program [OJJDP).

Lisa O. Barras, MA

Lisa Barrars an Associate Counselor, Associate Substance Counselor, and Certified Clinical Trauma Professional. She currently serves the Arizona Families First program as an EMDR specialized counselor. She has a passion for working with individuals with a history of trauma and substance abuse disorders. She also serves as an inpatient program therapist working with individuals diagnosed with depressive disorders, trauma related disorders, and substance abuse disorders. She received her Master's in Clinical Mental Health Counseling from Argosy University, Phoenix, Arizona with a focus in Forensic Psychology. Her research and clinical interests have focused on the specialized human growth and development of the juvenile population.

In: Juvenile Delinquency
Editor: Bonnie A. Nelson

ISBN: 978-1-63485-742-0
© 2016 Nova Science Publishers, Inc.

Chapter 3

COMPARATIVE JUVENILE RESTORATIVE JUSTICE: THE CASES OF ITALY AND CHILE

Claudia Reyes-Quilodran*[*]*, Catherine LaBrenz and Gabriela Donoso-Morales
Pontificia Universidad Católica de Chile, Santiago, Metropolitana, Chile

ABSTRACT

This research studies the construction of juvenile restorative justice in Italy and Chile, how these policies are implemented in practice, and how families participate in these processes. In-depth interviews were conducted with professionals about restorative justice in both countries regarding their experiences working both with policy and practice. The results show how Italians handled the main barriers to implement juvenile restorative justice programs, with suggestions for their implementation in Chile.

Keywords: restorative justice, juvenile offender, families

[*] E-mail: claudiar@uc.cl.

INTRODUCTION

Throughout the last few decades the concept of restorative justice has been introduced and restorative practices have been incorporated in various countries. Several authors (e.g. Christie 1977; Wright 1983; Braithwaite 1993) have written about the introduction and effectiveness of restorative justice, although restorative philosophies date centuries back. However, over the last 30 years in the Western world, the social movements of the 70s have also influenced the criminal justice system and the more traditional, punitive ways of dealing with conflict. The re-assessment of the position of several marginalized groups-namely women with the feminist movement, people of color with the civil rights movement and people with alternative sexual orientations-also led to both crime victims and perpetrators being re-considered. Christie (1977 p. 1) states, "*criminology to some extent has amplified a process where conflicts have been taken away from the parties directly involved and thereby have either disappeared or become other people's property*". The externalization of the conflict to the State or a third-party therefore discourages the parties involved from taking responsibility and really understanding the consequences of their actions. Hence, the introduction of restorative processes that might permit those involved to understand the harm caused, and take charge of their futures.

In 2001, the Council of the European Union agreed to create new strategies to encourage crime prevention. To achieve this objective it declared that all measures that are shown to reduce or otherwise contribute to reduce crime and citizens' feeling of insecurity, in this claim all the social and institutional actors, be invited to get involved in crime prevention. In this scenario, juvenile restorative justice appeared as an option of doing justice at different levels such as: victim-oriented, offender–oriented and place-oriented. Van Dijk and DeWaard (1991) explain that the Victim-Oriented approach focuses on the victim by conducting awareness campaigns to avoid being victimized, and increasing prevention for vulnerable groups. Moreover, it prevents repeat victimization by giving victim support once the crime is perpetrated and by repairing or compensating the victim's harm. The Offender-Oriented type focuses on implementing citizenship and educational programs, before the youth is involved in crime. It works with vulnerable youths that faced risk factors (Farrington 2000) leading them to be more susceptible to committing crimes or presenting violent behavior. The place-oriented looks for situational prevention by targeting environmental design and community-based intervention. It works to address antisocial behavior, neighbor watch and community mediation, identify high crime areas and implement community justice initiatives. Restorative justice involves community participation, and therefore, families should be directly or indirectly involved in the restorative process.

In Italy, restorative projects were first implemented in 2000 in different parts of the country with select mediation programs. Today, they passed a law decree which establishes the legal procedure for minors. This legal framework considers restorative justice as a tool to educate juvenile offenders. Even though they do not have a specific piece of legislation that refers to juvenile restorative justice like other European countries, Italian law permits the implementation of mediation programs. From 1996 to 2006, Italy presented a tendency to decrease the number of juveniles prosecuted and convicted (Harrendorf, Heiskanen and Malby 2010), and Italy has implemented innovative practices. The case of Italy is interesting to study due to the fact that in Italian culture, the extended family plays an important role in child raising and in family decision making. Moreover, people participate actively in community activities, resulting in higher levels of social capital and social cohesion (Putman 2000).

The objective of this research is to analyze the construction of restorative justice in Italy and Chile, how these policies are implemented in practice, and how families participate in these processes. Once these questions are answered, key barriers to the implementation of juvenile restorative justice program are analyzed, to provide a guiding framework for the adoption and implementation of restorative practices in Chile.

METHOD

As part of this investigation, ten professionals were interviewed in-depth about restorative justice in Italy and their experiences working both with policy and practice. From the group of interviewees, three were professionals who worked in three different mediation programs in three different areas; three were social workers from a juvenile probation program and educators from the same programs, one was a judge from the Minors Court, one was an official of the Ministry of Justice, and one was a psychologist from a semi-open program. Additionally, a monthly meeting of four mediators in the Victim Offender Mediation Program in Rome was observed, and a group interview was conducted regarding their experiences with specific cases. Additionally, various texts and publications about restorative justice in Italy were reviewed in an attempt to gain an understanding of the Italian context of restorative justice, how it is considered in Italy framework and how it is implemented in practice. Content analysis was used for the analysis (Paillé 2006).

In Chile, six professionals were interviewed in-depth about juvenile restorative justice and their experiences working in practice. These six professionals represented three different mediation programs in three different regions. As in Italy, various texts and legal instruments about juvenile justice system in Chile were reviewed.

RESULTS

In the following section, the Italian juvenile criminal justice system and Italian restorative practices are presented, and later the Chilean juvenile crime justice and Chilean restorative practices are analyzed in order to compare how these countries approach juvenile restorative justice and the impact that they have on the community and families.

ITALIAN JUVENILE CRIMINAL JUSTICE SYSTEM

In Italy, children who are 14-17 can be held responsible for crimes. Like most Western European countries, the goal of the juvenile justice system in Italy is to limit youth contact with the legal system. The youth's contact is perceived as a risk factor, because officials recognize that incarceration disrupts youth maturation and education. Italy passed the Juvenile Justice Procedural Reform Act of 1988 (Decreto del Presidente della Repubblica DPR 448/88) to require the Minor Court to consider diversionary tactics before ordering prison sentences. The Act established three methods of diversion. Judges can declare an offense irrelevant and dismiss it, issue a pardon if they believe the youth will not reoffend, or order *messa alla prova* ('putting you to the test'), which is essentially pre-trial probation. Judges can issue *messa alla prova* regardless of a youth's offense so that even murderers can serve pre-trial probation (Nelken 2006). The Minor Courts are in charge of overseeing the legal process as well as educative measures that are applied according to the juvenile's psychosocial needs. Here the prosecutor has an important role to determine the psychosocial problems affecting the youth in order to suggest the best sanction to the judge, to promote the well-being of the children. A social worker also makes formal suggestions that influence this decision. The judge is able to make a decision based on the psychosocial evaluation of the juvenile and her/his family group. The defense lawyer is practically absent due to the fact that the judge, prosecutor and social services are looking at the juvenile`s motivations to commit crime that are strongly related with risk factors that surrounding the youth.

The *messa alla prova* can take four to five years before the three judges apply a sanction. Even though this time is extremely long, the adolescents participate in a *messa alla prova* program, participating in an individual intervention program to improve the psychosocial conditions of the juvenile to reduce risk factors and promote protective factors to favor the adequate development of the youth and prevent crime recidivism.

Italian Juvenile Restorative Justice

There are different approaches to working in juvenile restorative justice. On the one hand, there are professionals who work with restorative justice in connection to crimes, where victims and offenders participate; other sorts of conflict are also incorporated into restorative practices-such as conflict in schools, and within communities-that may not necessarily constitute a crime. This group of professionals works in mediation programs and advocates restorative justice not just as practices and policies, but rather as a philosophy to embrace that promotes autonomy, responsibility and empowerment of each individual to take control of his or her own life. Others include a restorative justice approach in the intervention program with the juveniles. For example, the probation programs and *messa alla prova,* as well as the semi-open programs have one of the intervention's objectives oriented to promoting responsibility and making the adolescent take responsibility for damage caused.

Italian Mediation Programs

Youth enter the juvenile justice system when the police arrest an offender under 18 years of age. When the police detain the adolescent, they are required to inform the juvenile prosecutor and social services to follow the penal process. The prosecutor evaluates the evidence to determine if the youth will be prosecuted, while social services begin the psychosocial evaluation and inform the judge and prosecutor to determine *messa alla prova*. At this time, juveniles are able to voluntarily attend a mediation program with the judge's order, and the prosecutor is able to send the youth to mediation center.

In 1997, Law 285 was enacted, and several organizations participated in the implantation of mediation programs. In 2000 they signed a protocol, in which different agencies committed their financial support for mediation centers. Five mediation centers were implemented in five different regions. The mediation centers received financial support from different sources. The public agencies are supported by the Minor Center of Justice, Minor Court, Prosecutor office and Municipality. The private program, like the Palermo Mediation Center, is financed by the Institute Don Loncalabrio and the University of Palermo. All of them follow the United Nations' Guidelines for Restorative Justice (United Nations 2006). There is an average of twelve professionals per team. For instance, Palermo Mediation Center has 5 psychologists, 2 lawyers, 1 sociologist, 2 social workers, and 2 educators. The mediation centers also work with a group of volunteers who have had training in mediation. The team works in school mediation, juvenile restorative justice and gives training in mediation to sensitize the community. During a one-year period, the mediation centers work with approximately 80 juveniles. The Ministry of Justice in Rome monitors the centers and offers training.

The mediation centers conduct Victim Offender Mediation (VOM), which involves a perpetrator who has confessed or partially-confessed to a crime, the victim, and a mediator. The mediation process takes place between one victim and one offender (sometimes with the option of accompaniment by parents). The mediator has the first interview with the offender to evaluate if s/he is able to participate in the mediation process, has the ability to communicate and if (s)he regrets what s/he did. The family members are able to participate in this process too. The second interview is with the victim, the objective is to inform her/him about the mediation process and confirm if s/he wants to participate. They set the mediation meeting, in which two mediators, the victim and the offender participate. Both victim and offender can be accompanied by their parents. This is a *direct mediation*, where each part expresses how they experienced the offense, the offender apologies, and a written agreement is signed by both parties. The mediator follows up to ensure that the agreements were met, and informs the judge or prosecutor. The *indirect mediation* occurs when the victim does not want to meet with the offender. The victim is able to write a letter to express how s/he feels and how the offense affects her/him, and the offender answers this letter under the supervision of the mediator. In some cases, community service can be developed. This case will be sent to another office in charge of the community service, because a social worker will do the follow up, so that the offender attends and concludes the actions (for example, visiting an elderly home for two months and reading to them).

The mediation centers work with school mediation. They work with resolving school conflicts and conducting interviews with the different parts involved in the conflict, and implementing the mediation process if the parts want to do it. They use this instance to prevent crime, making the school community involved in the conflict resolution.

ITALIAN JUVENILE PENAL PROGRAMS

During the *messa alla prova* and the sanctions' programs (probation and semi-open centers), the individual intervention plan for juveniles is implemented, and includes restorative justice elements. This plan is led by the juvenile and the social worker. The Juvenile Justice Procedural Reform Act of 1988 states that the juvenile has not completed his/her full maturity and requires an educative intervention in order to prevent him/her from perpetrating crimes again in the future. Under this umbrella, restorative justice is viewed as an educative tool, in which the youth has to be responsible for what s/he has done and repairs the damage caused. Most of the cases do community service, and this activity is supervised by the social worker in charge of the case. The social workers interviewed stated that this procedure helps the youth to perceive their own actions and see the consequences of the harm caused by them. It is important to highlight that restorative actions are only one of the objectives of the intervention plan; there are other objectives oriented to improving the psychosocial conditions of the juveniles and favoring their adequate development.

All the professionals interviewed coincided about the characteristics of the families who attend these programs. One group belongs to the lower class, they live in a poor neighborhood and present family problems like drug addiction, domestic violence, unemployment and juveniles report previous crimes. Nevertheless, the other group is regular families, who belong to the middle class and sometimes lower classes, but they do not present the social problems that the other group does. Youth in the latter group tend to be referred on their first crime, and generally the juvenile perpetrates minor crimes such as lesions, threats, verbal aggressions, or thefts.

Chilean Juvenile Crime System

In Chile, like Italy, children who are 14-17 can be held responsible for crimes. Chile passed the Juvenile Justice Law 20.084 in 2007. This coincided with Chile signing the International Convention on the Rights of the Child of 1990, requiring the international community to adopt measures in favor of childhood, especially for juvenile offenders. This law requires the Criminal Courts (Tribunales de Garantía) to be in charge of juvenile crime process. Each Criminal Court has to implement a specialized room, and the public prosecutor and public defense attorney should also be specialized in childhood. Nevertheless, the courts have limited specialized rooms for juveniles. The Criminal Courts are in charge of conducting the legal process and social reinsertion, rehabilitation, and making the youth responsible for his/her actions. The penal sanctions are applied mainly based on the seriousness of the crime and previous records, like adult penal procedure, regardless of the juvenile's psychosocial needs. Here, the prosecutor has an import role to collect evidence about the crime, while the defense attorney tries to discredit the evidence and reduce the degree of the crime and reduce the sanction. The psychosocial problems which affect the youth are not relevant. Occasionally, the judge asks for a specialized team's recommendation from an Ambulatory Diagnosis Center (DAM). Once the sentence is stated, the National Service of Minors (SENAME) is in charge of carrying out the sanction. SENAME is responsible for the direct administration of juvenile prisons and semi-closed programs. The ambulatory sanctions such as probation, community services, and reparation of damage are administered by private agencies that are under SENAME′s supervision. The maximum sanction that a youth can receive is ten years in prison. The law focuses on a socio-educative approach that promotes the social insertion and rehabilitation of the juvenile offenders.

Chilean Juvenile Penal Programs

In Chile, two forms of juvenile restorative justice are implemented: Community service and reparation of damage. Both programs are implemented by private agencies. The Option Corporation is the only agency that drives the program to repair damage, and this agency has four programs in different regions; each program has two professionals in charge of the reparation of damage (a social worker and a psychologist). The interviewees indicate that they receive 5 to 6 cases per year, and explain that prosecutors and judges do not apply this sanction very often; despite the fact that the team has had meetings with the judges to explain the benefits of this sanction. The professionals have participated in brief trainings about restorative justice practices, and they implement direct mediation using VOM. The program for reparation of damage has faced several problems, including the low numbers of cases sent by the court, and the long distances that the professionals must travel to contact the juveniles. They spend 3 hours or more per day traveling from their workplace to the juvenile´s residence. The professionals cover a large distance, with a spread-out population. This makes it difficult to follow-up the cases and sees the impact of the program. Additionally, the same professionals oversee cases sent to the community service program. Each professional has approximately 20 cases, and they have to formulate an intervention plan with the juvenile offender. Because the juveniles have to complete a specific amount of hours of community service, the social worker evaluates the youth's personal interests and coordinates with an public or private agency where the juvenile participates doing some tasks.

The profile of the juveniles who participate in both programs is broad: some of them have high criminal involvement, and for others it is the first time that they have had contact with the criminal justice system. The participation of the family is very limited, because the sanction focuses mainly on the juvenile. Chile does not have any mediation center for juveniles in conflict with the law, and restorative practices are very limited. One of the explanations for this is that the Chilean legal system is highly punitive. Moreover, the different juvenile programs do not follow up with their cases and they do not evaluate the impact. These features make it difficult to perceive which are the best measures and practices for the juveniles and how the intervention plan impacts youth offenders.

CONCLUSION

The experience of juvenile restorative justice in each country is very different. In the case of Italy, it is possible to observe that the community and the families' participation in the restorative process is an important piece of the program's success. The professionals indicate that the restorative process produces effects in family culture. They mention that in the Italian culture, revenge (vendetta) is allowed as form of conflict resolution, and this method increases conflict and violence. When mediation practices were implemented in Sicilia and Torino, the team is able to perceive that violence decreased and people began to incorporate restorative practice as a legitimate way to resolve conflicts. Restorative justice permits families from different socioeconomic background to participate and to be directly involved in what is going on with their children. The main barrier that Italians had to overcome was the authorities' support for their implementation and financial support for mediation centers. The strategy used to achieve their sponsor was to create alliances with universities to offer training and resources.

The Italian juvenile penal system states that youth contact with the criminal justice system is a risk factor that makes them more vulnerable to violence and criminal exposure. Moreover, when youths belong to families with complex needs, the risk factors make relapse more probable. Under this scenario, restorative practices are an alternative to prevent the juvenile and her/his family from being exposed to the criminal justice system, and gives the families a chance to handle the juvenile violent behavior early-on. The Italian praxis allows one to learn different approaches to reduce violence and criminal conduct in the context of a larger society.

Even though Chile does not have a complete comprehension of juvenile restorative justice and its impact on the larger community, there is a growing group of people that is seriously interested in implementing these practices, and learning from international experience. Another aspect from Italian culture that Chileans have to look at is that Italians have Minors Court for the juveniles, and Chile had a very similar system until 2007 when Law 20.084 was passed. Since then, the Chilean penal system for youths does not consider the bio-psychosocial problems that these juveniles face daily, because it does not look at the risk factors that motivate young people to perpetrate crimes.

The Chilean legal system's answer is punitive, and the sanctions do not necessarily respond to the juvenile's' needs, and finally social problems are penalized. On the other hand, the Italian approach puts the youth's' needs as a core for the psychosocial intervention plan and their families participate in this process, which gives them the chance to repair the damage and its consequences.

References

Braithwaite, J. (1993). Pride in Criminological Dissensus. *Law and Social Inquiry, 18,* 501-512.

Christie, N. (1977). Conflict as Property, *British Journal of Criminology*, *17,* 1-15.

Convention on the Rights of the Child. (1990) Adopted and opened for signature, ratification and accession by General Assembly resolution 44/25 of 20 November 1989 entry into force 2 September 1990, in accordance with article 49.

Decreto del Presidente della Repubblica DPR 448/88 (1988). Approvazione delle disposizioni sul processo penale a carico di imputati minorenni.

Farrington, D. (2000). Explaining and Preventing Crime: The globalization of knowledge, *Criminology*, *38*, 1-24.

Harrendorf, S., Heiskanen, M. and Malby, S. (2010). International Statistics on Crime and Justice. European Institute for Crime Prevention and Control Affiliated with Nation United. HUINICH, 64.

Ley 20.084. (2007). Establece un Sistema de Responsabilidad de los Adolescentes por Infracciones a la Ley Penal. Congreso Nacional de la República de Chile.

Paillé, P. (2006). La méthologie qualitative. Postures de recherche et travail de terrain. Paris: Armand Colin.

Putman, R. (2000). Bowling Alone: The Collapse and Revival of American Community. SAGE, New York.

Nelken, D. (2006). Italian Juvenile Justice: Tolerance, Leniency or Indulgence? *Youth Justice*, *6* (2), 107-128.

United Nations (2006). Manual sobre Programas de Justicia Restaurativa. United Nations Office on Drugs and Crime. New York.

Van Dijk, J., and DeWaard, J. (1991). A two-dimensional typology of crime prevention projects: With a bibliography. *Criminal Justice Abstracts,* 483-503.

Wright, M., (1983). Making Good: Prisons, Punishment and beyond. *The Journal of Criminal Law and Criminology, 74,* 1635-1638.

Biographical Sketch

Name: **Claudia Reyes-Quilodran**

Dr. Reyes-Quilodran received her PhD from Washington State University in 2009.

Her areas of specialization include political psychology, criminal justice and Latin American studies. Her most recent research projects include juvenile delinquency and gender; professional judgment and decision- making in the intervention with vulnerable families; and comparative studies in juvenile restorative justice.

She has a long experience working with victims affected by severe human rights violations during the Chilean military regime, and she has worked in the state agencies to prevent crime and violence in Chile.

Affiliation: Assistant Professor. Social Work School. Pontificia Universidad Católica de Chile

Education: Social Work, MA in Criminal Justice, Ph.D. Political Science

Address: Avenida Vicuña Mackenna 4860, Campus San Joaquín, Macul, Santiago, Chile.

Research and Professional Experience:

2015-2016 *Compassion Fatigue and Hazards of Working in Child Welfare/Juvenile Justice and Child Mental Health Settings.* The study focuses on exploring how social workers in Chile and in the United States address compassion fatigue when working in fields such as child welfare, juvenile justice and child mental health.

This research is conducted with the School of Social Work at University of Michigan.

2013-2014 *Fondecyt N° 13201* 'Professional Judgment and decision making with families affected by complex needs. This research studies the categories that define the social workers′ perceptions of the families in the Child Protection Services.

2010- 2014 *Marie Curie Actions, FP7-PEOPLE-2009-IRSES. Research project:* Understanding and Supporting Families with Complex Needs International research exchange programme to address a recognized deficit in family focused research by developing links between divergent disciplines and knowledge streams, both nationally and internationally. There search has been developed by Professor Reyes-Quilodrán in Milan, Italy, to know the implementation of juvenile restorative justice.

2010 – 20013 *Inicios.* The endogenous and exogenous factors that influence the juvenile offenders to perpetrate crime. The results contributed to the practitioner to know the causes of the criminal behavior rand how they have to work with the juvenile offenders and their families.

2009-2004 *World Bank* Mac Namara Foundation, The factors that determine the torturers behavior, contributed to identify the motivations and individual, group and institutional influences to prevent future human rights violations.

Professional Appointments:

08/09-Present: Assistant, Professor. School of Social Work, P. Universidad Católica de Chile.

07/06-Present: Coordinator and professor of post graduate study "Certificate in Social Intervention with Juvenile Offenders." Universidad Católica de Chile, School of Social Work.

03/07-03/09: Researcher in the Study Department of the National Server of Minors.

03/05-02/06: Part time Professor, School of Social Work, Universidad Alberto Hurtado, Santiago Chile. Design and Statistic analysis of the National Survey "School Violence."

05/03-12/03: Data analysis, Washington State Division of Governmental Studies and Services.

01/00-05/03: Teaching Assistant of the curse: Comparative Political Science, American Government Systems, Comparative Criminal Justice Systems, Control System in Criminal Matters, and Organizational Management and Evaluation. Department of Political Science and Criminal Justice, Washington State University.

Summer 2002: Internship in the American States Organization (ASO), Inter-American Commission of Human Rights. Washington D.C.

Summer 2001: Internship in the United Nation Organization (UN). Human Right Commission. Geneva. Swiss.

09/96-03/94: Director and Social Worker of the Mental Health Program for victims affected by political violence (PRAIS). South Service of Health. Ministry of Health. Chile.

01/92-03/94: Social Worker of Child Welfare program. National Service of Minor. Chile.

Honors:

Visiting professor University of Michigan 2015 – 2016

Member of the Honorific Society of Political Science Pi Sigma Alpha, USA.

Outstanding graduate students. Department of Political Science and Criminal Justice at the Washington State University.

Publications Last 3 Years:

Reyes, C. (2014). ¿Por qué las adolescentes chilenas delinquen? Revista de Política Criminal. Vol. 9, 17, 1-26.

Reyes, C. (2014). The Chilean socioeconomic crisis and political violence in 1973. Chapter of book. Tra fede e storia. Studi in onore di don Giovannino Pinna, AIPSA Fondazione Mons. Giovannino Pinna. Editores "Martino Contu, Maria Grazia Cugusi, Manuela Garau, "Quaderni della 3. Cagliari 2014, pp. 251-268. ISBN: 978-88-98692-15-6.

Reyes, C. (2014). El por qué de la conducta delictiva de adolescentes chilenas recluidas. Revista 93. Mujeres y Sistema Penal, Número 11, año 6, Diciembre 2014, p.p. 34-41. Defensoría Penal Pública.

In: Juvenile Delinquency
Editor: Bonnie A. Nelson

ISBN: 978-1-63485-742-0
© 2016 Nova Science Publishers, Inc.

Chapter 4

YOUTH TRANSITIONS AND SOCIAL EXCLUSION: AN EMPIRICAL STUDY OF YOUNG EX-OFFENDERS' REINTEGRATION IN CHINA

Haoyue Zhang*
Department of Applied Social Sciences,
City University of Hong Kong, Hong Kong

ABSTRACT

Youth crime is one of the most critical issues faced by many countries around the world, and it has been identified as a significant national problem for China's ongoing social transition. Youth crime is not only related to many other social problems but also triggers a series of moral crises in society. The Chinese government, social service organizations, and local communities have been trying to devise a comprehensive, effective system to tackle the issues of disorderly behavior and youth crime (Wang, 2006). However, these researchers and practitioners overemphasize prevention and punishment of youth criminal behaviors, rather than focusing on the rehabilitation and reintegration of young offenders. In China, such a misplaced emphasis has led to high recidivism rates and relevant social problems. Therefore, this chapter

* Corresponding author: Department of Applied Social Sciences, City University of Hong Kong, Kowloon, Hong Kong. Email: haoyzhang8-c@my.cityu.edu.hk.

aims to obtain a general understanding of the crime-desistance transitional life and social reintegration experiences of young ex-offenders. Specifically, an exploratory, qualitative study was conducted to investigate the social exclusion that four young ex-offenders experienced when they re-entered Chinese society. Their own and relevant stakeholders' experiences and views were analyzed. Three themes around reintegration and social exclusion—social ties and support; social discrimination and labeling; and opportunities to education, training, or work—were derived from the interviews and discussed on the basis of criminological and sociological theories (social support theory, labeling theory, and human and social capitals). Relevant implications and recommendations are provided for academic thinking and policy making.

Keywords: young ex-offender, reintegration, social exclusion

INTRODUCTION

With a population of around 1.3 billion, China is the largest developing country in the world. Chinese society has been changed since 1949, and the pace of change has been rather remarkable since the "Reform and Opening-Up" policy was implemented. Along with the rapid pace of social change, Chinese society is currently facing a series of opportunities and challenges. On the one hand, they have made social progress and improved technical advancements. On the other hand, to some extent, they have interfered with social stability and social order. In China, the number of juvenile offenders sentenced to prison each year more than doubled from 2000 to 2008 to almost 89,000 (The Economist, 2013), and youth crime has accounted for approximately 70–80% of the total criminal offences in recent years (Ministry of Justice, PRC 2009). According to a survey report by the Communist Youth League of China (2014), some new conditions and problems have emerged, for instance, a lower average age of young offenders and rising violent crime. In addition, more rural children and young people are committing crimes; this includes both young migrants in cities and around 60,000,000 youngsters left behind by parents who have migrated to work in urban areas (The Economist, 2013). In Henan Province, more than 70% of juvenile offenders came from rural areas in 2013 (Dahe, 2014). Evidently, dealing with youth crime has become one of the most significant issues in Chinese society, attracting much attention.

There are many studies and policies on delinquency and crime-prevention work, such as the Law of the People's Republic of China on the Prevention of Juvenile Delinquency (1999) issued by the Standing Committee of the National People's Congress. However, upon release from prison and re-entry into society, young ex-offenders are still one of the most neglected and vulnerable groups. The Universal Declaration of Human Rights (1948) states that all human beings are born free and equal in dignity and rights, which means that everyone, including young ex-offenders, should be treated equally and have equal access to education, work, housing, health services, and so on. However, the reality of Chinese society is that young ex-offenders are always labeled as a special group and treated unequally (Zhang, Wang and Huang, 2011). In particular, traditional Chinese culture emphasizes the importance of "face" and "reputation," which means that people's past greatly influences others' impressions of them and thus their future life. For a long time, no relevant regulation or law protected young offenders' criminal records and privacy in China, until the amendment of Criminal Procedure Law in the beginning of 2013 (Hu, 2013). Therefore, even with the Chinese government's stance that young ex-offenders should have equal opportunities in education and employment, they still face much discrimination and social exclusion given their past. Unfortunately, this, in turn, leads to their negative attitudes toward social life and often to deviant behavior, even re-offending (Wang, 2010).

Therefore, this research in this chapter uses qualitative methods to investigate and explore the transitions and social exclusion that young ex-offenders experience when they are reintegrated into Chinese society, taking into account their own and relevant stakeholders' experiences and perspectives. Then, the findings are analyzed and linked to some implications and suggestions for further academic thinking, policy making, and rehabilitation practice.

Conceptual and Theoretical Contexts: Social Exclusion and Young Ex-Offenders' Reintegration

Conceptualization of Social Exclusion

The term "social exclusion" is now widely employed in many research areas: social science, politics, and economics. According to Kabeer (2005) and

Mathieson et al. (2008), the concept of social exclusion appeared for the first time in the 1960s in France, but it was the rising unemployment and income inequalities during the economic crisis of the 1980s that helped it gain currency in many European countries. With considerable economic and social dislocation, European countries were then dealing with massive challenges of globalization in their labor markets and welfare states. Therefore, at that time, the European Foundation offered a relevant definition of social exclusion:

> Social exclusion is a process through which individuals or groups are partially or wholly excluded from participation in the society where they live (Kabeer, 2005).

Given its origins and rapid spread across nation states and global regions, the phrase "social exclusion" has inevitably been used in different ways at different times, reflecting different institutional, political, historical, and geographic contexts. According to Fish (2003), social exclusion became a prominent item on the European Union's (EU's) policy agenda in the late 1990s. The concept also became a key interest in policymaking and practice in the United Kingdom (UK) following the establishment of the Social Exclusion Unit in 1997 by the New Labour Government. From then on, both governments and academics paid more attention to defining and specifying the concept of social exclusion.

According to Percy-Smith (2000), the European Commission has provided a quite comprehensive definition of social exclusion in the report Social Exclusion—Poverty and Other Social Problems in the European Community:

> Social exclusion refers to the dynamic and multidimensional factors resulting in individuals or groups being excluded from the normal rights, practice and exchanges of modern society. Except for poverty as an obvious factor, social exclusion also refers to the inadequate rights in housing, health, education and access to services. It leads to social discrimination and separation, and it emphasizes the weaknesses in the social infrastructure and the risk of forming a two-tier society (EU Commission, 1993).

This definition is very comprehensive and useful because it not only emphasizes the multiple factors related to social exclusion but also refers to its profound influence on the whole society. However, it does not specify "the deliberate effect of law and politics as in the case of prisoners, asylum seekers and refugees" (Cruells and Igareda, 2005).

Silver (1994) identifies three paradigms that she argues embed different meanings and usages of the term social exclusion. First, the Solidarity paradigm, embedded in French Republican political ideology, views social exclusion as the breakdown of cultural and moral social bonds between individuals and society. Second, the Specialization paradigm, influential in Anglo-American liberal thought, holds that social exclusion is a form of social discrimination rooted in unenforced rights and market failures. Third, the Monopoly paradigm, drawing on the European Left thought, regards social exclusion as the result of the formation of group monopolies that restrict outsiders' access to sources (Silver, 1994). Silver's analysis on the concept of social exclusion has provided multiple perspectives and approaches for understanding its nature and causes. However, her views have been heavily drawn on advanced Western democracies and are primarily concerned with political ideologies underpinning the definitions of social exclusion, so their applicability in the modern global context still remains to be examined (Mathieson et al. 2008).

On the basis of Silver's theories, Levitas (2005) identifies three different discourses in regard to social exclusion in the UK, illuminating how the ideological underpinnings for concepts of social exclusion change over time and how these discourses influence relevant social policies or actions. First, Redistribution Discourse (RED) regards social exclusion as the consequence of poverty and low income, so the income levels of the poor should be raised and their access to public and private services should be improved. Second, Social Integrationist Discourse (SID) attributes social exclusion to unemployment and unpaid work, so labor market participation must be increased. Third, Moral Underclass Discourse (MUD) focuses on the moral and cultural causes of social exclusion and argues that there is an "underclass" and a "dangerous class"—including, for example, young offenders and lone parents—that are detached from mainstream society (Levitas, 2005). Although these three discourses are highly focused on the established social welfare system and practical situations in the UK, they can also be used as a reference in other nations and districts. Besides, Levitas et al. (2007) devise a comprehensive working definition of social exclusion:

> Social exclusion is a complex and multi-dimensional process. It involves the lack or denial of resources, rights and services, and the inability to participate in the normal social relationships and activities

which are available to the majority of people in the society, no matter in economic, cultural, social or political fields. It can affect both the quality of life of individuals and the equity and cohesion of society as a whole (Levitas et al. 2007).

Overall, the various definitions of social exclusion offered by governments and academics support Room et al.'s (1992) views on the concept of social exclusion. He posits that social exclusion should be conceptualized as a multidimensional, dynamic, and relational process. On the one hand, it represents the rupture of bonds between individuals and society, resulting in a lack of social participation and social integration; on the other hand, it can be understood as a product of social relationships that assign different social identities and associated power and status to different individuals and groups.

Young Ex-Offenders' Social Reintegration and Social Exclusion in China

The concept of social exclusion was introduced in China for the first time in 2000. Since then, its use in social research in China has become increasingly popular, especially with respect to the research of vulnerable groups. As there are numerous differences in social structure, culture, and history between the West and China, the roots of social exclusion and its development in China possess their own characteristics. However, less social exclusion research has been conducted on young ex-offenders' transitional lives and social reintegration. The following passages cite several relevant studies on young ex-offenders, social reintegration, and social exclusion.

Gao and Zhang's (2013) study on ex-offenders' social adaptation reveals five factors that may influence the process and outcome of adaptation: (1) individual factors, (2) peers, (3) families, (4) community, and (5) national policies. Wang (2010) specifies the issues involved in juvenile offenders' social adaptation after their release from prison. She mentions that the traditional custodial prison correction approach makes it difficult for young offenders to reconnect with mainstream society and assimilate social development, and such difficulties may, in turn, lead to recidivism. She also analyzes the psychology, interpersonal relationships, and economic adaptation of young offenders after they are released, indicating that improving their self-cognition, reducing social discrimination and labeling, developing a social support network, and providing necessary training and career opportunities can contribute to their adaption to society and reduce re-offending. Zhang et al.'s (2010) research on the social support for young ex-offenders suggests that as a special vulnerable group, young ex-offenders have experienced social exclusion and discrimination because of their previous offending history. Obstacles arise in their path of re-socialization and increase the possibility of re-offending. Moreover, Chinese people put extreme emphasis on "face" and "reputation," further aggravating labeling of ex-offenders and influencing their employment, relationships, and social life. Hu's (2012) study reveals that young ex-offenders face social exclusion in four aspects: economics, politics, public services, and social relationships. For instance, they have limited career choices and are excluded from positions in state organs, face unequal treatment in social welfare and health services, and are disregarded or discriminated against by their families and community members. Gao (2010) and Lin (2008) both analyze the common types of social exclusion in Community Correction. The former researcher divides social exclusion into three levels: the social exclusion implied in national legislations and social policies, the social exclusion in social service organizations and job centers, and the social exclusion from community and family members (Gao, 2010). The latter researcher asserts that the social exclusion during Community Correction is influenced by the factors of family, education, employment, community, and social welfare. On the basis of previous research, Jing (2012) summarizes the roots of social exclusion faced by young ex-offenders, including the traditional Chinese "kin-oriented network"; undeveloped civil society; the lack of relevant legislation; and social discrimination in the labor market, social networks, and even among family members.

The array of studies described in the preceding passages on youth transitions and reintegration after release from prison or under community supervision have identified and generated many significant topics and factors related to social exclusion, such as social relationships, social support, discrimination and limited resources and opportunities. However, most studies lack relevant sociological and criminological theoretical underpinnings that explain the causality of social exclusion. Only a few theories grapple with the concept of social exclusion at this level, for example, social support theory (Cullen 1994), labeling theory (Lemert, 1972), and human and social capital theory (Bourdieu, 1986; Burt, 1992; Coleman, 1988, 1990; Lin, 2000; Portes, 1998; Putnam, 1995; Woolcock, 2001). According to Maruna and Immarigeon (2004), ex-offenders' reintegration is both an event and a process. Narrowly speaking, re-entry comes the day a prisoner is released from confinement. In its own way, the time (or timing) of a prisoner's release offers challenges and conflicts that may or may not be managed by correction officials or criminal justice agents." Therefore, this exploratory research not only examines the components and factors of social exclusion in young ex-offenders' transitional lives but also analyzes the causality and process of social reintegration and exclusion from relevant theoretical perspectives.

Research Method and Sample

In accordance with the aims this chapter, a qualitative research method was adopted to explore the factors and causes of social exclusion facing young ex-offenders in China through several semi-structured interviews with both young ex-offenders and relevant stakeholders. Semi-structured interviews are based on a prepared interview guide that includes some general questions on specific topics (Becker, Bryman, and Ferguson, 2012). Although some questions were devised in advance, they were viewed as interview clues instead of strict structures, so considerable flexibility was present, with the interviewers able to modify the order of questions and specific wordings used in asking questions to probe for elaboration. Additionally, the interviewees were encouraged to provide active answers and elaborate on their own perceptions and experiences. Thus, semi-structured interviews are likely to involve several dialogues. Besides, compared with other research methods, semi-structured interviews focus more on targeted individuals or groups and can therefore obtain more effective responses that contribute to in-depth information and better understanding (Payne and Payne, 2004).

Regarding the sampling method, the researcher adopted a purposive sample of young ex-offenders and stakeholders in China. Jiyuan and Yangcheng, two small cities in Henan Province and Shanxi Province, respectively, were chosen as the sampling sites. Henan Province has the largest and most fluid population in China, whereas Shanxi Province is famous for its pristine traditional Chinese culture and folk customs. First, the researcher contacted some staff members from two relevant agencies in the two Provinces, namely, the Committee for the Wellbeing of the Youth and the Juvenile Criminal Prosecution Department of the People's Procuratorate present in both Jiyuan, Henan Province and Yangcheng, Shanxi Province. Both of the agencies in Jiyuan and the Committee for the Wellbeing of the Youth in Yangcheng consented to the interviews. However, the Juvenile Criminal Prosecution Department of the People's Procuratorate in Yangcheng rejected the request owing to their local agency's rules. The Committee for the Wellbeing of the Youth is a nationwide social organization, funded by the Chinese government, working with young people, especially young ex-offenders. The Juvenile Criminal Prosecution Department of the People's Procuratorate is one department of the national organization for legal supervision that focuses on juvenile crimes. Then, the semi-structured interviews with three staff members of these agencies were conducted. Through these interviews, we can not only learn about the local experts' views on the research subject but also negotiate access to a sample of young ex-offenders for interviews. After the introduction and permission of the stakeholders from the agencies, four young ex-offenders aged between 14 and 25 were selected from Jiyuan and Yangcheng as the sample of the main semi-structured, qualitative interviews. Because one interviewee among the sample was under 18 years old, the researcher first contacted his parents to obtain consent for his participation. Then, four interviews were conducted separately with the young people. To illuminate the findings of these semi-structured interviews, a combination of biographical narrative and inductive, exploratory thematic analysis was chosen to analyze and identify the key information collected.

When conducting social research, especially with young people, ethical issues and risk assessment should be considered carefully (Noret, 2011). Conducting this empirical research required ethical approval from both Durham University and the agencies that helped the researcher gain access to the participants. Along with the ethical approval, research participants must be fully informed about the research and then their informed consent must be obtained (UCL Research Ethics Committee, 2013). Therefore, every participant was provided with an information sheet and a consent form in both English and translated Chinese versions for illuminating the following: purpose and process of the study, their right to withdraw without penalty at any point, why they are invited, what will happen if they participate, audio-recording and transcribing of the interviews, ensured anonymity and confidentiality, and the researcher's contact details. Before their participation, potential participants were allowed to ask relevant questions about the research. Only then were they asked to read and sign the forms. In addition, research involving children and young people under 18 years old must first gain informed consent from their parents or guardians.

FOUR CAMEOS OF YOUNG EX-OFFENDERS IN HENAN AND SHANXI

Participant A: Male, 16 years old, currently studying in high school; previous offence: public security.

Participant A was born as the only child in a local wealthy family. He was somewhat spoiled by his parents and grandparents, as he said, "No matter what I want, they (his family members) will get it for me." A's parents sent him to study in one of the city's best high schools even though his academic achievement and performance in school was mediocre. However, he took pride in his high prestige among his fellow students because he was regarded as a rich and privileged boy at school, but then he became acquainted with many delinquent friends and gangs. In 2013, one of his classmates from a poorer family borrowed money from him and promised to repay him with a usurious interest rate. However, the classmate was unable to pay A, even with A repeatedly asking for the money. A became so angry that he asked some of his friends to beat up the classmate. In response, the classmate who had borrowed money asked others to beat up A. A asked his friends to beat up the classmate again, and this time, the classmate suffered a perforated eardrum. He called the police, and A was arrested along with some of his friends. Since A's parents offered to pay for the damages and A was under 18 years old, he was ordered to join a one-year project of community-based correction in his own community. Now, he has returned to school but is monitored every day and must regularly participate in several voluntary social services. During the interview, he said that he hated school and studying because his academic performance was poor and most of his teachers and classmates knew about his delinquent past. Therefore, he would rather hang out on the streets with friends than go to school. He was apprehensive about the college entrance examination in the upcoming year because his parents pressured him too much. He was looking forward to finding a job, with the help of his parents, as soon as possible after graduation from high school.

Participant B: Male, 24 years old, currently unemployed; previous offence: larceny and robbery (twice).

Since he was very young and his parents had to work all year in a far-off city, Participant B was raised by his grandparents in a rural village. He sees his parents only once every two or three years during the Chinese Spring Festival. He believed that his parents cared little about him and even regarded him as a shame after he was arrested. He loved and respected his grandparents but had difficulty communicating with them since they were too old to understand his feelings. Nine years ago, as a 15-year-old boy, he received an extremely poor score in his high school entrance examination and had no hope of entering any regular high school; he could only attend a technical or a specialized school. During the summer vacation then, he had nothing to do but hang out in the village or spend time in a costly Internet cafe. His grandparents were not financially secure, and he was unwilling to take a part-time job. Under such testing circumstances, he stole bikes during that summer and sold them to get money. Consequently, he was arrested and sentenced to three years in a "Re-education through Labor" programme, established by the Department of Ministry of Public Security. He was released at 18 years old without any higher education or work skills, so he could not find a job. Besides, he was always discriminated against and refused by the recruiters because of his past as a young-offender. He gradually became frustrated and again became addicted to online computer games. Caught in a vicious cycle, he committed a robbery once again and spent a 5-year sentence in prison till 2016, when he was released early for good behavior. Although he was 24 years old, he was still unemployed and continued living with his grandparents. He became involved in a relationship in 2016, but his girlfriend's parents opposed the relationship because of B's unemployment and criminal history. He was learning to drive and preparing to work in a small private transport company operated by one of his friends. He was determined not to commit crimes anymore, and he intended to have a family with his girlfriend in the future. In addition, he planned to move his family, along with his grandparents, from the village to a city when he earned enough money because he felt stressed living in a small village, with a bad reputation and could not find a satisfactory job because of the limited opportunities there.

Participant C: Male, 22 years old, currently unemployed; previous offence: intentional injury (gang crime).

Participant C grew up in a rural area, and all his family members were farmers. He had experienced extended unemployment after leaving high school. In the spring of 2013, he found employment as a production-line worker in a manufacturing industry in a city near his hometown. His earnings were satisfactory, but his work was quite monotonous. He was frequently required to work overtime, so he could not see his family and had no time to find a girlfriend. The only leisure in his daily life was having a drink with some co-workers who also worked far from home. Although these drinks over dinner were mostly innocuous, on one occasion, one of the co-workers talked the relationship problems he was experiencing with his girlfriend because of another man's interference. In their inebriated state, the young people decided to fight the unacquainted man on behalf of their friend. They beat up the man, whose eyes were seriously injured by C. The police arrested the group of drunk co-workers involved in the scuffle, and C was later sentenced to one year's suspended prison sentence for the crime of intentional injury. At the time of this study, he had been released from prison for a probationary period. He was dismissed at work because of his criminal record. He relied on part-time jobs to make a living in the city and did not want to return home because he felt his family members might be heartbroken and frustrated with him. He deeply regretted his impulsive, inebriated actions and wanted to immediately start his life afresh.

Participant D: Female, 18 years old, currently in the community-based correction system; previous offence: drugs charges.

D was a young girl from a divorced family, and both her parents had started their own families. Therefore, she had lived with her grandparents for a long time since she was very young. She started to live in the school dormitory after entering middle school and gradually made some friends outside of school. She felt that these friends liked and cared about her more than her family did because they helped her skip classes, invited her to eat delicious food, have a drink, sing karaoke, and even bought beautiful clothes for her. She liked to call them her "older sisters" to show that she regarded them as family. Two years ago, one of her "older sisters" asked her to meet several people in a hostel room and introduced them to her. After chatting for a short time, they asked her to taste "something good," and she just tried a bit without exactly knowing what it was. Later, they told her that she had tried drugs, but she did not refuse trying some more. A hostel staff member caught them in the act, and the police arrested them. Because she was under 18 years old and it was her first offense, she was given an opportunity to join the community-based correction project for one year. On the future, she said, "I want to leave my hometown and find a job in the south of China, maybe in Guangzhou or Shenzhen. I cannot find a job here because everyone knows about my past and gossips about it. Anyway, my parents never care about what I am doing or where I am going because they have their own life. I want to be a good girl and live for myself in the future."

FINDINGS AND DISCUSSIONS

Lack of Social Ties and Support

When the four young ex-offenders talked about their lives after their release from prison or the correctional system, they all mentioned the significance of familial and social relationships in everyday life. They mentioned a lack of support from their family, the community, and the government during the re-entry period:

> "My parents left home to work in a city when I was very young, and we rarely meet except during the Chinese Spring Festival. My grandparents raised me, but now they are discriminated against by their neighbors because of my offending past … I want to start a stable family with my girlfriend, but her parents oppose our relationship because I have committed a crime." [Participant B]

> "I don't want to go back home because I don't want to face my family members. I will feel extremely sad if they are disappointed about my mistake." [Participant C]

> "Some of my old friends are still serving their sentences in prison, so I have lost contact with them. My parents got divorced when I was young and have started their own new family, so they don't care about me anymore. I have nobody to talk to—only a friendly social worker who often visits me and talks with me during the process of community correction. She has helped me a lot." [Participant D]

Moreover, the workers from the Committee for the Wellbeing of the Youth and the Juvenile Criminal Prosecution Department of the People's Procuratorate also talked about the relevant support they provided for young ex-offenders and the problems confronting their practice:

> "We did a lot of investigations into the family backgrounds of these young offenders/ex-offenders when we dealt with the youth criminal cases, so we can consider their situations and provide proper help, such as free law aid services … Community correction is operated and supervised by the local Justice Department only." [Stakeholder 1]

> "The staff members in our agency, including the retired teacher, experts, veterans, and cadres, volunteer to communicate with young offenders/ex-offenders and offer free psychological counseling and skill training for them." [Stakeholder 2]

> "We did provide some support services and organize several activities for young ex-offenders through cooperating with other government organizations, communities, and schools in the past few years, but we don't have enough financial support to provide these services regularly, and most of the previous activities did not achieve a great effect." [Stakeholder 3]

When asked about whether they have received any feedback about their services and activities from young people, all three workers answered "no."

The discourse above exemplifies young ex-offenders' relationships with their families and friends as well as the influences of familial and social support on their experience of social exclusion. In fact, social relationship is a central notion in Chinese culture and traditions. According to the Differential Mode of Association (Chaxu geju) in China proposed by Fei (1985), in the Chinese society, an individual is surrounded by a series of concentric circles produced by that person's own social influence. Each larger circle becomes more distant and more insignificant. Everyone's circles are inter-related, and a person touches different circles at different times and places. On different occasions, an individual's own social network comes into contact with someone else's (Fei, 1992). Since "consanguinity" and "proximity" are the most important criteria of relationships in Chinese society (Fei, 1992), people attach great importance to their closest social relationships. Therefore, relationships with families, relatives, friends, co-workers, or neighbors, as well as the support from them, play a significant role in young ex-offenders' reintegration into society. However, the increasing divorce rate in contemporary Chinese society triggers the breakdown of numerous family relationships (China Daily, 2014); at the same time, the imbalanced levels of economic development in Chinese urban and rural areas force many rural laborers to migrate to cities, leaving many rural children behind (BBC, 2010). Therefore, many young ex-offenders from such family patterns lack necessary affective and instrumental support from their closest relations.

The importance of social support in young ex-offenders' reintegration has been widely discussed (Chung, Little, and Steinberg, 2005; Cobb, 1976; Coleman, 1988, 1990; Cullen, 1994; Jin, 2014; Liu and Chui, 2014). Cobb

(1976) establishes three categories of social support, including emotional support, esteem support, and mutual obligations, and claims that necessary social support could increase coping ability and facilitate adaptation into the changed environment. Cullen (1994) defines social support as social integration within group relationships in which individuals provide mutual social, emotional, and material support. Coleman (1988) demonstrates that social capital, in the form of supportive family and community bonds, is strongly associated with young people's well-being and development. Chui and Cheng (2014) assert that the need for social support is more salient for young offenders than that for adults. Social support is not only significant for young ex-offenders' reintegration but also beneficial for their transition from youth to adult life (Chung, Little, and Steinberg, 2005, cited in Chui and Cheung, 2014). However, in China, the relevant social security and social services systems are not well established; in fact, young ex-offenders find it difficult to obtain the necessary social support even on the macro level. As the relevant stakeholders mentioned, although some social services have been provided for young ex-offenders by the government and other organizations, they cannot develop these services persistently because of a lack of funding. Consequently, they cannot achieve satisfactory outcomes. In addition, China's community correction is operated and supervised by the Justice Department rather than by professional social workers, so their intervention work lacks scientific methods and cannot provide adequate, satisfactory support (Lin, 2008). Moreover, the inequalities between urban and rural areas of the Chinese social security system and social insurance system also contribute to the exclusion of young ex-offenders in rural areas (Li, Sato, and Sicular, 2013).

Social Discrimination and Labeling

According to our interviews, social discrimination and labeling are pervasive issues faced by young ex-offenders. These issues are present in varying forms and can affect various aspects of their life after prison.

Participant A complained about discrimination and isolation in his new school life:

> "All the teachers and classmates know about my past. They make remarks on my history and always regard me as an 'evil' boy. I hate school life."

Participant C lost his previous beloved job because of his criminal act, and he was rejected when he tried to apply for the same job again. He said,

> "My previous employer refused my application this time because I have a criminal record and am still supervised in the probationary period. Many other companies refused me for similar reasons. I can only find some low-paying, temporary jobs in the city."

The other two young offenders also mentioned their unpleasant experiences of being isolated and discriminated against in their daily life when they tried to re-enter society and begin a new life.

> "My reputation isn't good in my village because of my criminal history, so I am always despised by other villagers. It makes me feel that I have to 'hang my head' when I walk on the streets. I cannot find formal work in the village, and my girlfriend's parents don't allow her to get into a relationship with me—an ex-offender." [Participant B]

> "The neighbors always make remarks about me and ask their children to stay away from me because I used to be a drug abuser. That makes me feel ashamed and lonely. Anyway, I want to leave my hometown and live in a southern city where nobody knows me." [Participant D]

Addressing the issue of social discrimination against young ex-offenders, a worker at the Juvenile Criminal Prosecution Department of the People's Procuratorate said,

> "Juvenile offenders used to face much discrimination and exclusion when they tried to re-enter society because of their criminal record and history of imprisonment ... Since the newly revised Criminal Procedure Law was adopted in March 2013, the phenomenon of discrimination has decreased. Newly established mechanisms, such as minors' conditional non-prosecution mechanism and the criminal record sealing mechanism, do contribute to juvenile offenders' rehabilitation rather than their imprisonment and punishment." [Stakeholder 1]

The young ex-offenders' views make it clear that they have experienced a common feeling of being labeling and discrimination against in many aspects of daily life, such as school life, career development, neighborhood relationships, etc., because of their criminal history. Chinese people place great importance on one's "reputation" and "face," so once a person becomes an offender or ex-offender, he or she is forever negatively labeled (Jin, 2010). Such a culture not only causes inequality in opportunities and rights but also adversely affects young ex-offenders' self-esteem and social identity. These unfair, negative factors tend to increase their frustration, make them hostile to society, and increase the possibility of re-offending (Zhang et al. 2010). George Herbert Mead (1934) uses the concept of symbolic interaction to describe the importance of the meaning that people attach to the messages they receive through communications with other people. For Mead, an individual's self-image is shaped by his or her interactions with others through a period of time, often referred to as the looking-glass self (Cooley, as cited in Don Martindale, 2013). From the symbolic interaction perspective, labeling theory was developed. This group of theories calls attention to the role that society's reaction to delinquency might play in influencing subsequent delinquent behavior. According to Lemert's (1972) discourse on primary and secondary deviance, although labeling theory might not be able to explain young people's first criminal acts, how their parents, friends, teachers, or law enforcement agencies react to those first acts does, in fact, greatly influence their subsequent behavior. Once young people feel singled out as "bad kids," they may internalize that label, and it becomes a self-fulfilling prophecy. In other words, young people might begin to act according to the label that has been attached to them. Braithwaite (1989) argues that individuals are so enmeshed within interlocking segments of the local community that the only way they can ever become law-abiding, contributing citizens is when a sense of communitarianism exists. He uses the word "shaming" to describe a process whereby the local community lets the offenders know that it disapproves of their behavior, and this message is intended to make offenders see the error of their ways. If, however, the process is stigmatizing, as opposed to reintegrative, young people could be driven even further down a path toward delinquency and crime.

According to the stakeholder quoted above, before March 2012, there were no regulations or laws in China that addressed the protection of juveniles' privacy and reintegration after their release from prison or correctional facilities. More attention was paid to the prevention and punishment of youth crime than to young ex-offenders' rehabilitation. Therefore, life after release became a "nightmare" for young ex-offenders, and they faced social exclusion and discrimination due to the imprisonment and lifelong criminal record (Dong, 2006). After the establishment of minors' conditional non-prosecution system and criminal record sealing mechanism, young offenders who have committed minor crimes can be placed into the community-based correction system instead of being imprisoned. Also, an offender under 18 years old at the time of the crime will be sentenced to less than 5 years of imprisonment (Criminal Procedure Law of the PRC, 2012). These legal reforms may contribute to a reduction in the discrimination and exclusion faced by young ex-offenders and help them better reintegrate into society. Despite these changes, in reality, labeling of and prejudice against young ex-offenders still exists to a certain degree, especially in their most familiar environments.

Lack of Opportunities to Education, Training, and the Labor Market

To adapt to mainstream society more smoothly and build a better future, most young ex-offenders would like to re-enter schools, join training programs, or find employment in the labor market. However, reality cannot meet their expectations, and they are confronted with many barriers in accessing appropriate education, training, and employment. Participant A described his torturous experience in school life:

> "Although I have returned to my previous high school, I am not happy at all. I cannot catch up with other students and always get poor grades. All the teachers and classmates know my past. I hate school life."

The other young offenders also talked about their unpleasant experiences and feelings during the process of finding a job:

> "I am unemployed now because I cannot find a job in the local area. I plan to learn some skills and find a job in other places, like car repairing." [Participant B]

> "My previous employer refused my application this time. Many other companies refused me … I can only find some temporary and low-paying jobs in the city." [Participant C]

> "I know that I cannot pass the College Entrance Examination because I didn't get any formal education in all these years." [Participant D]

One employee of the Committee for the Wellbeing of the Youth presented several services they had offered to help young ex-offenders resume their education or find a satisfying job:

> "We tried to cooperate and reach agreements with some companies and agencies. They agreed to provide more work opportunities for young ex-offenders. The staff members in our agency volunteer to offer free psychological counseling and skill training for them." [Stakeholder 2]

According to Articles 23 and 26 in the Universal Declaration of Human Rights (1948), everyone has the right "to education, to work, to free choice of employment, to just and favorable conditions of work and to protection against unemployment." However, in contemporary China, because of the labeling of former criminal behavior and the fear of crime arising from social insecurities, many opportunities in education, training, and work are not accessible to ex-offenders. For example, China's Civil Servant Law (2005) stipulates that anyone who has been subjected to criminal punishment cannot be employed as a civil servant. In reality, many companies and agencies tend to promptly refuse job applicants with a criminal record. On the one hand, this behavior arises from the prejudice and discrimination against ex-offenders; on the other hand, many young ex-offenders lack essential educational achievement and work skills as they are sentenced to custody at a relatively young age. Also, young ex-offenders are always not welcomed by many common schools and training institutes because of the fear of their negative impact on the other students (Lin, 2008). Even though some young ex-offenders return to school, they experience an unpleasant school life because of poor academic performance and exclusion by peers.

The exclusion from education, training, and employment not only harms ex-offenders' self-esteem and social belonging but also decreases human- and social-capital development during their transition into society. Human capital, defined by skills and qualifications, is considered a key determinant in gaining employment or for progress at work (Brook, 2005). In recent years, social capital has been recognized as an additional determinant that can significantly influence young people's development. Social capital is generally viewed as resources that inhere in relationships among actors and that facilitate a range of social outcomes (Coleman, 1990). The extent to which individuals either contribute to or experience social trust, norms, reciprocity, or civic participation can influence a range of important personal outcomes, including education and employment. Recent research indicates that social capital is not only a critical input for education but also one of its valuable byproducts (Coleman, 1988, 1990; Heyneman, 1998). In the context of employment, social capital—bridging and linking social capital in particular—can be seen as a positive asset for those seeking to find or change jobs in the labor market (Burt, 1992; Lin, 2000; Portes, 1998; Woolcock, 2001). Community-based correction agencies, social work organizations, community members, and governments should work together to achieve effective bridging and linking between young people and to provide more opportunities for them to participate in social activities.

CONCLUSION

This chapter has explored the social exclusion facing young ex-offenders in their transitional and re-entry life through semi-structured interviews with them and also with stakeholders. According to a relevant literature review and these research findings, many young Chinese ex-offenders are experiencing social exclusion during their transitional period, mainly because of a lack of social ties and support; limited access to education, training, and work; and social discrimination and labeling. The findings are analyzed based on relevant theories and social policies, such as social support theory, labeling theory, and social capital theory. Several implications for further policy making and practice are listed below:

- Families, friends, co-workers, and community members should provide essential, emotional, and instrumental support for young ex-offenders, communicating with them frequently. Both statutory and voluntary sectors should design and provide more accessible social services for young ex-offenders to support their reintegration into society. These include employment information and counseling services; more professional officers, social workers, and volunteers should involve themselves in community-based correction practice. The government should provide more funding and material resources for relevant social service organizations.

- Schools and labor markets should provide equal opportunities for young ex-offenders and avoid labeling them and discriminating against them. More basic education and practical skill training programs should be introduced in custody or prison to avoid young offenders' alienation from mainstream society and to help them re-enter society more smoothly after their release from prison (Wang, 2010).
- To curb labeling of and social discrimination against young ex-offenders in education, the labor market, and social life, relevant national organs should earnestly implement the minors' conditional non-prosecution system and criminal record sealing mechanism. At the same time, mass media should report youth-offending cases more objectively and properly to reduce the public's misunderstanding and demonization of young ex-offenders (Hu, 2009).

This study in this chapter has two main limitations. First, the research samples are relatively small. Interviewees included only four young ex-offenders and three stakeholders from two agencies in two small cities. Therefore, our findings might not be representative of metropolitan areas or remote rural areas. Second, youth crime and social exclusion are quite sensitive topics and some interviewees might feel uneasy talking about such issues with an unfamiliar person; as a result, they might conceal some information. Furthermore, the researcher conducted the study as an "outsider," trying to avoid any personal influence on qualitative research. However, as a young Chinese person, the researcher might also have latent sympathy when conducting interviews with young ex-offenders.

REFERENCES

Becker, S., Bryman, A., and Ferguson, H. 2012. Understanding Research for Social Policy and Social Work: Themes, Methods and Approaches. Bristle: The Policy Press.

Bourdieu, P. 1986. "The Forms of Capital." Handbook of Theory and Research for the Sociology of Education, *edited by* John G. Richardson, 241–258. New York: Greenwood Press.

Braithwaite, J. 1989. Crime, Shame and Reintegration. *Cambridge:* Cambridge University Press.

BBC. 2010. "China to Address Economic Imbalance." Accessed August 9, 2014. Available at: http://www.bbc.co.uk/news/world-asia-pacific-11548719.

Burt, R. S. 1992. Structural Holes: The Social Structure of Competition. Cambridge, MA: Harvard University Press.

China's Civil Servant Law. 2005. (issued by the Standing Committee of the National People's Congress). Accessed July 3, 2014. Available at: http://www.lawinfochina.com/display.aspx?lib=law&id=4123&CGid=.

Chui, W. H., and Chan, H. C. 2012. "An Empirical Investigation of Social Bonds and Juvenile Delinquency in Hong Kong." *Child & Youth Care Forum 41(4):*371.

Chung, H. L., Little, M., and Steinberg, L. 2005. "The Transition to Adulthood for Adolescents in the Juvenile Justice System: A Developmental Perspective." In On Your Own Without a Net: The Transition to Adulthood for Vulnerable Populations, *edited by* D.W. Osgood, E.M. Foster, C. Flanagan, and G.R. Ruth, 68–113. Chicago, IL: University of Chicago Press.

Cobb, S. 1976. "Social Support as a Moderator of Life Stress." *Psychosomatic Medicine* 38(5):300–314.

Coleman, J. S. 1988. "Social Capital in the Creation of Human Capital." *The American Journal of Sociology 94:*S95–S120.

Coleman, J. S. 1990. Foundations of Social Theory. Cambridge, MA: Bellknap Press.

China Daily. 2014. "Marriage Crisis in China? Divorce Rate Rises across the Country." Accessed July 3, 2014. Available at: http://www.chinadaily.com.cn/hkedition/2014-01/24/content 17255014.htm.

Cruells, M., and Igareda, N. 2005. Women, Integration & Prison. Barcelona: Aurea Editores.

Cullen, F. T. 1994. "Social Support as an Organizing Concept for Criminology: Presidential Address to the Academy of Criminal Justice Sciences." *Justice Quarterly 11(4):*527–559.

Dong, L. 2006. "Community-Based Correction and the Re-Socialization of Young Offenders." *Neijiang Technology 6:*36–42.

Fei, X. 1992. From the Soil: The Foundations of Chinese Society. Oakland, CA: Univ of California Press.

Fei, X. 1985. From the Soil: The Foundations of Chinese Society. Beijing: SDX Joint Publishing Company.

Fish, J. 2010. "Conceptualising Social Exclusion and Lesbian, Gay, Bisexual, and Transgender People: The Implications for Promoting Equity in

Nursing Policy and Practice." *Journal of Research in Nursing* 15(4):303–312.

Gao, M., and Zhang, Y. 2013. "Foreign Research on Ex-convicts' Social Adaptation and Its Revelation for Contemporary China." Journal of East China University of Science and Technology (Social Science Edition) 1:32–42.

Hagan, J., and Bill, M. 2010. "*Social Capital and Crime.*" In Encyclopedia of Criminological Theory, *edited by* F. Cullen, and P. Wilcox, 425–428. Thousand Oaks, CA: SAGE Publications.

Hu, C. 2012. "New Regulations of Youth Crime in the Latest Criminal Procedure Law." Hunan Agriculture 5:27.

Jin, L. 2010. "*On the Reconstruction of Social Support Network about the Community Correction Objects—A Qualitative Research on a Community Services in Shanghai.*" PhD diss., China Youth University for Political Sciences, Beijing.

Kabeer, N. 2005. "Social Exclusion: Concepts, Findings and Implications for the MDGs." *Paper commissioned as background for the Social Exclusion Policy Paper*, Department for International Development (DFID), *London.*

Law of the People's Republic of China on the Prevention of Juvenile Delinquency. 1999. Accessed May 3, 2014. Available at: http://www.lawinfochina.com/display.aspx?lib=law&id=4852&CGid

Lemert, E. M. 1972. Human Deviance, Social Problems, and Social Control. Englewood Cliffs, NJ: Prentice-Hall.

Levitas, R. 2005. The Inclusive Society? Social Exclusion and New Labour (Second edition). Basingstoke: Palgrave Macmillan.

Levitas, R., Pantazis, C., Fahmy, E., Gordon, D., Lloyd, E., and Patsios, D. 2007. The Multi-Dimensional Analysis of Social Exclusion. Bristol: University of Bristol.

Lin, L. 2008. "*Social Exclusion of the Object and the Intervention of Social Worker.*" Master's Thesis, Central China Normal University, Beijing.

Liu, L., and Chui, W. H. 2014. "Social Support and Chinese Female Offenders' Prison Adjustment." *Prison Journal* 94(1):30–51.

Lin, N. 2000. Inequality in Social Capital. Contemporary Sociology 785–795.

Martindale, D. 2013. *The Nature and Types of Sociological Theory* (Vol. 11). New York: Routledge.

Mathieson, J., Popay, J., Enoch, E., Escorel, S., Hernandez, M., Johnston, H., and Rispel, L. 2008. "Social Exclusion Meaning, Measurement and Experience and Links to Health Inequalities." A Review of Literature. WHO Social Exclusion Knowledge Network Background Paper, 1.

Maruna, S., Immarigeon, R., and LeBel, T. 2004. "Ex-Offender Reintegration: Theory and Practice." In After Crime and Punishment: Pathways to Ex-Offender Reintegration, *edited by* S. Maruna and R. Immarigeon, 152–180. Cullompton: Willan Publishing.

Mead, G. H. 1934. Mind, Self, and Society. Chicago: University of Chicago Press.

Ministry of Justice, P. R. C. 2009. Research Institution of Crime Prevention: The Trend of Youth Crime Needs Dialectical and Scientific Analysis. Accessed May 6, 2014. Available at: http://www.moj.gov.cn/2008rdgz/2009-11/16/content 1182344.htm.

Noret, N. 2011. Guidelines on Research Ethics for Projects with Whildren and Young People. Accessed May 4, 2014. Available at: http://www.yorksj.ac.uk/pdf/Guidelines%20in%20Research%20Ethics%20for%20Projects%20involving%20Children%20and%20Young%20People.Pdf.

Payne, G., and Payne, J. 2004. Key Concepts in Social Research. London: Sage.

Percy-Smith, J. 2000. Policy Responses to Social Exclusion. Buckingham: Open University Press.

Portes, A. 1998. "Social Capital: Its Origins and Applications in Modern Sociology." *Annual Review of Sociology* 24:1–24.

Putnam, R. D. 1995. Bowling Alone: America's Declining Social Capital. *Journal of Democracy* 6(1):65–78.

Room, G., Berghman, J., Bouget, D., Cabrero, G. R., Hansen, F., Hartmann-Hirsch, C., and Vranken, J. 1992. Observatory on National Policies to Combat Social Exclusion. Second Annual Report. Brussels: Directorate General for Employment, Social Affairs and Industrial Relations, Commission of the European Communities.

Silver, H. 1994. "Social Exclusion and Social Solidarity: Three Paradigms." *International Labour Review* 133:531–578.

The Economist. 2013. Juvenile Crime: Hard Times. Accessed August 25, 2014. Available at: http://www.economist.com/news/china/21588402-how-young-criminals-are-treated-says-much-about-urban-rural-gap-hard-times.

UCL Research Ethics Committee. 2013. Guidance Note 1: Research Involving Children. Accessed May 4, 2014. Available at: http://ethics.grad.ucl.ac.uk/forms/guidance1.pdf.

United Nations. 1948. The Universal Declaration of Human Rights. Accessed May 3, 2014. Available at: http://www.un.org/en/documents/udhr/.

Wang, D. 2006. "The Study of Juvenile Delinquency and Juvenile Protection in the People's Republic of China," *Crime and Justice International* 22(94):4–5.

Wang, Y. 2010. "*Study on Social Adaptation of Juvenile Offenders out from Prison.*" Master's Thesis. Qingdao: Shandong University of Technology.

Woolcock, M. 2001. "The Place of Social Capital in Understanding Social and Economic Outcomes." *Canadian Journal of Policy Research* 2(1):11–17.

Vaismoradi, M., Turunen, H., and Bondas, T. 2013. "Content Analysis and Thematic Analysis: Implications for Conducting a Qualitative Descriptive Study." *Nursing & Health sciences 15(3):*398–405.

Zhang, Y., Wang, Z., and Huang, S. 2011. "Environment Support for Young Ex-Offenders' Re-Socialization." *Youth Crime* (1):29–32.

Reviewed by Xuan NING. Department of Applied Social Sciences, City University of Hong Kong, Kowloon, Hong Kong. Email: xning6-c@my.cityu.edu.hk.

INDEX

A

D

G

H

I

J

L

M

N

O

P

Q

R

S

T

U

V

W

Y